50 Buildings that Built Wales

MARK BAKER GREG STEVENSON DAVID WILSON

GRAFFEG

Key

Kilometres
0 10 20 30 40 50 60

Miles
0 10 20 30 40

SNOWDONIA
NATIONAL PARK

PEMBROKESHIRE COAST
NATIONAL PARK

BRECON BEACONS
NATIONAL PARK

GOWER

WALES

ENGLAND

N

Contents

Cover photograph: Tredegar House, Newport by David Wilson.   * No fixed location

Preface

These are the buildings that built the modern Welsh nation; the structures that formed our sense of what Wales means, and what the country and her people are.

We had a difficult task whittling our long list of influential buildings down to a mere fifty. A few were such obvious contenders that we couldn't leave them out, whereas others are included more as a representative sample of a building type that has helped to form Welsh identity. We could easily have filled a book with 'Fifty Influential Welsh Chapels' or 'Fifty Castles that Changed Welsh History', but in order to give balance and make for a visually interesting and engaging read we've necessarily had to limit our selection. We've also generally avoided buildings outside of Wales, though it could be argued, for example, that the Palace of Westminster has had significant influence on the shape of modern Wales. That said, we couldn't resist including a Patagonian example to remind readers of how the Welsh diaspora also informs our national identity. In the difficult cull down to just fifty buildings we also said goodbye to 'buildings' which are no longer extant like RAF Penyberth on Penllyn which boosted Welsh nationalism in the 1930s after it was the victim of an arson attack.

Please remember as well that this isn't a book of 'Fifty Very Welsh Buildings'. Most of the structures selected aren't, in fact, peculiar to Wales, even if they are built of local materials in local styles. A few are even pattern-book examples that could have been constructed anywhere in the British Isles, or possibly even the world. We propose these buildings as our selection of structures that represent the history that has formed modern Wales and our understanding of Welshness.

Here, then, are buildings built by the Welsh, for the Welsh, and sometimes even against the Welsh such as Caernarfon Castle. Yet even that famous castle has, over time, become an icon of Welsh, rather than English, heritage. This is the wonderful thing about nationhood, it is defined by the people and has fluid edges that are hard to describe. For that reason we've also included the bridge at Llanfarian and the lost structures at Capel Celyn, Tryweryn, both sites associated with popular protest that, over time, have come to strengthen our sense of nationhood and culture.

Ultimately, this is a personal selection. We each know the buildings that make our own Wales. Even if you disagree with a few of our choices, we hope you'll consider the case we make for each, and enjoy reading the fascinating histories they embody. We hope, too, that you will reflect on your own 'Buildings that Built Wales'. As architectural historians it is inevitable that we have chosen buildings we know and love. But we also know that each reader will have a favourite chapel, a traditional cottage, a farmhouse, a favourite view of a castle, an industrial site that are no less valuable than ours in defining Wales to them.

Everyone has an individual relationship with our country, but we hope this book brings together a collection of rich histories that we can all agree have helped make Wales the wonderful and meaningful place that it is today.

Mark Baker and Greg Stevenson

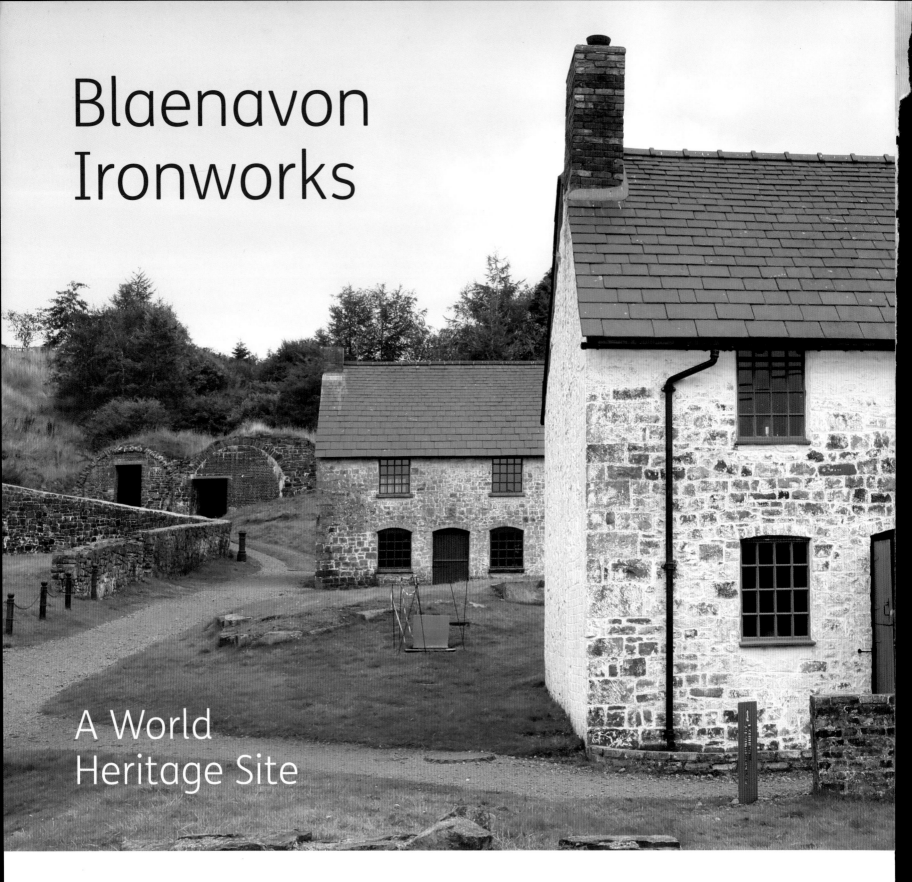

Blaenavon
Ironworks

A World
Heritage Site

Wales was the first industrial nation in the world. By 1850 more people in Wales were employed in industry than in agriculture, and the mineral deposits that lay under the surface of the Welsh landscape made it rich, as it developed into a land of heavy industry and mass employment. Through mass emigration to Wales, the population rose from just under 600,000 in 1801 to around 2,000,000 by 1901. Internal migration saw many people move from rural locations to the south-east, settling around Cardiff, Swansea, Newport and the Valleys.

Welsh iron was used all over the world, from ship's cannons to the railways of Europe, Russia and America. In 1787 Lord Abergavenny leased his land to three businessmen; Thomas Hill, Benjamin Pratt and Isaac Pratt, and, in 1789, the production of iron began at Blaenavon. The topography of the land was important as the furnaces needed to be built into a slope so that the brick and stone chambers could be fed from above. A mix of ore, coke and limestone were fed into the interior of the furnace where jets of air fired the temperature to great heights to produce molten iron. This was tapped off into sand moulds in the casting house built adjacent to the furnace. The workers, many of whom had come from an agricultural background, likened the rivers of iron travelling through the sand to piglets feeding from a mother sow. With this in mind, pig iron was named.

Three blast furnaces were constructed at a total cost of £40,000, a huge sum to outlay for a new method of production.

Blaenavon Ironworks

People: Lord Abergavenny; Thomas Hill, Benjamin Pratt and Isaac Pratt; Sidney Gilchrist Thomas and his cousin Percy Gilchrist.

Place: In 1787, Lord Abergavenny leased his land at Blaenavon to three businessmen and, in 1789, the production of iron began. Blaenavon Ironworks is now a museum and World Heritage Site.

Event: Blaenavon Ironworks testifies to Wales' role as the world's first industrialised nation. The basic steel-making process was later invented here by Sidney Gilchrist Thomas and Percy Gilchrist.

The people who lived in these houses kept the furnaces burning night and day to ensure production was continuous

The ironworks were crucial in the development of producing cost-effective iron ore for a mass market. Novelist Alexander Cordell set his famous book, *Rape of the Fair Country*, at the ironworks and contributed to getting the site statutory protection. Reality television took over the Stack Square cottages in 2007 and 2008 for two series of *Coal House*, a production in which families experienced and relived life in the south Wales coalfield in the 1920s and 1940s. Participating families had to live in authentically furnished and functioning dwellings, and the cottages they used are now open to the public.

The eighteenth-century blast furnace is one of the best surviving examples of its kind in the world. It is also one of the earliest, making it a site of international importance. The workers who kept the furnaces burning night and day to ensure production was continuous were housed in Stack Square, a residential area contemporary with the building of the original furnaces. Ever at the forefront of innovation, modern day techniques of steel production were pioneered at Blaenavon during the 1870s.

The site at Blaenavon continued to produce iron until 1904 and survived as a coal yard until the 1960s. With great foresight, the local council presented the ironworks to the Ministry of Works, now Cadw, for preservation. The furnaces are presented in various stages of dereliction which allows the visitor to see how they functioned. The ironworks are an integral part of the Blaenavon World Heritage site, and are reminders of Wales' status as the world's first industrial nation.

Penrhyn
Castle

Everything at Penrhyn was oversized and presented a forbidding appearance in the landscape

Pennant family and Edward VII at Penrhyn Castle 1894.

Penrhyn Castle

People: Owners Richard Pennant (1737-1808) and then George Hay Dawkins-Pennant (1764-1840); architects Samuel Wyatt (1737 – 1807) and then Thomas Hopper (1776–1856).

Place: Penrhyn Castle is a substantial nineteenth-century country house in the style of a Norman castle.

Event: Pennant made his fortune from Jamaican sugar and from slate quarries in north Wales. High quality slate from these quarries was exported worldwide.

Slate, money and extravagance are words which can easily be used to describe Penrhyn. The riches of the slate industry were poured by the Pennant family into the Penrhyn estate, and so proud were they of their source of income they had a bed of slate made for Queen Victoria's visit in 1859. Originally a medieval manor house which had been granted a licence to crenellate, Penrhyn survived relatively untouched until the 1780s.

Samuel Wyatt was employed by Richard Pennant to remodel his family seat at Penrhyn, near Bangor in 1782. Richard had entered Parliament as MP for Petersfield in Hampshire in 1761 and maintained a parliamentary seat for

nearly twenty years. He inherited Penrhyn in 1781 and quickly commissioned Wyatt to modernise the old manor house. Wyatt had been employed across the Menai Straits by the Williams-Bulkeleys to remodel the Jacobean mansion of Baron Hill, Beaumaris in 1776. At Penrhyn, as at Baron Hill, Wyatt used the structure and plan of the original house as a point of reference in his design. The cellars were retained together with the medieval circular staircase turret; although altered, the great hall was converted into a centrally entered entrance hall, placed in the centre of the now symmetrical U-shaped house. Castellations were added to match the surviving tower and to bring harmony to the whole design and the detached medieval chapel was

moved a few hundred feet away from the new house in order to become part of the landscaped park. Wyatt, most unusually, used yellow mathematical tiles hung on the exterior walls in order to resemble brick. Wyatt's Penrhyn did not survive for long, and was then entombed within Thomas Hopper's vast Norman edifice, built for George Hay Dawkins-Pennant between 1820 and 1838.

Hopper's Penrhyn was built on a palatial scale, rivalling the Bulkeley's mansion at Beaumaris and the Hughes' home at Kinmel. Everything at Penrhyn was oversized and presented a forbidding appearance in the landscape. The Norman keep dominates the bailey layout of the rest of the building complex, and it was in

the keep that the Pennant family's private apartments were situated. It reputedly cost the family £150,000 to build and then furnish.

The Penrhyn Slate Quarry at Bethesda was one of the main sources of income for the estate and employed over three thousand quarrymen at its peak in the 1890s when it was the world's largest slate quarry. Two industrial disputes, in 1896 and 1900-03, have gone down in history as being markers in the British Labour Movement. Workers went on strike for better pay and safer conditions and the market virtually collapsed as the north Wales slate industry was unable to cope with meeting demand. Thousands of workers were laid off and Penrhyn Castle

became a symbol of hatred in the bitter dispute.

The National Trust took over in 1951 and opened the castle to the public. The art collection boasts works by Canaletto, Rembrandt and Richard Wilson. Today, Penrhyn is one of the Trust's most popular visitor attractions in Wales and, with new partnerships with Bangor University, the story of the castle and the Pennant family is being further explored. The austere neo-Norman architecture may not be to everyone's taste but it is unique in Britain and a physical reminder of the wealth of the slate industry which made Wales one of the biggest industrial players in the world.

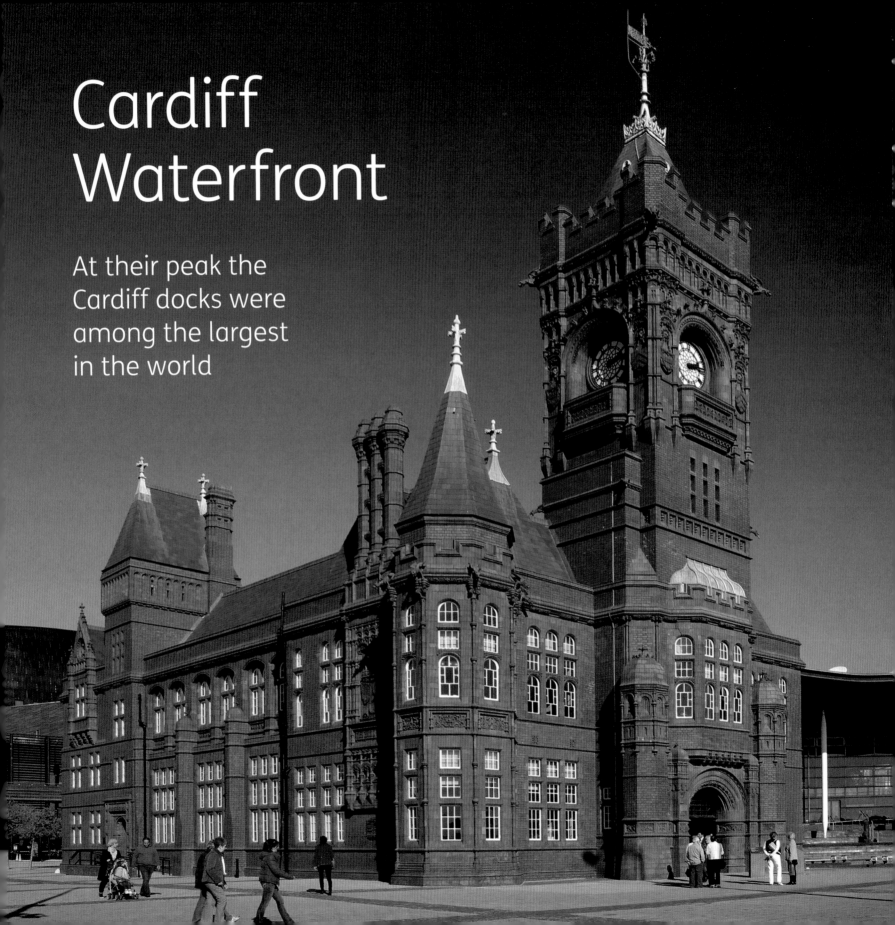

Cardiff Waterfront

At their peak the Cardiff docks were among the largest in the world

It might appear vain to name a town after oneself, but Butetown, the dockland area of Cardiff, really can be attributed to the Marquesses of Bute. The area is named after John Crichton-Stuart, Second Marquess of Bute who built a model housing estate there and was the man who developed the docks and encouraged iron and coal exports. He's often termed the 'father of modern Cardiff'. His son of the same name, the Third Marquess (1847-1900), developed the docks further and oversaw their tremendous success in the late nineteenth century.

At their peak, the Cardiff docks were among the largest in the world with almost 11km of quayage, second only to nearby Barry in terms of the amount of coal exported (some 10.7 million tons in 1913). Coal fuelled the industrial revolution that was transforming every country in Europe, and Wales had a mechanism to extract good quality coal and to distribute it to these centres of change. In this sense, Wales became a powerhouse of Europe, a status reflected in the handsome late Victorian buildings of Butetown.

The immense wealth of the Third Marquess of Bute left Wales with an enriched architectural heritage in gentry buildings such as Cardiff Castle and Castell Coch, but the wider influence of his coal and export industries is visible across much of south-east Wales. Coal and iron created improved transport links and also encouraged the construction of terraced workers' housing in the industrialised valleys. These rows of uniform nineteenth-century terraces with slate roofs, tightly packed against the sides of steep green valleys, have become an internationally recognised symbol of Welsh architecture.

The dockland area that has more recently been rebranded as Cardiff Bay was an important, not to mention wealthy, administrative area for the export of minerals and the import of goods that were indirectly funded by Welsh industry. The late Victorian and Edwardian buildings around Mount Stuart Square were among the finest built in Britain in their day. They reflect an architectural confidence that Wales has largely lost since, and were built with budgets that would be rare today. In the late 1800s Cardiff was every bit the equal of, say, Liverpool or Dublin, and it is no surprise to see that it constructed buildings of a quality that reflected this.

The Cardiff Coal Exchange was built between 1883 and 1886 to a design of Seward & Thomas architects on the site of the central gardens of Mount Stuart Square. It is a handsome piece of late Victorian architecture, built in a style loosely based on French Renaissance designs and constructed in Corsham cream limestone. Coal owners, ship owners and their agents would congregate in the main trading hall to negotiate prices and contracts. The atmosphere was akin to a modern-day trading floor for stocks and shares, with a couple of hundred men gesticulating and shouting. At one time the price of the world's coal was determined at the Coal Exchange.

The Coal Exchange has an interior that befits the most important commercial building in Wales of its time. Inside are sumptuous Jacobethan rooms that mix

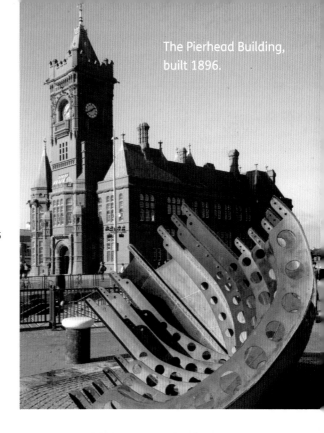

The Pierhead Building, built 1896.

Cardiff Waterfront

People: John Crichton-Stuart, Second Marquess of Bute (1793-1848); architect William Frame.

Place: Cardiff Docks, Coal Exchange, Pierhead Buidling and the Wales Millennium Centre.

Event: At the forefront of today's flagship Cardiff Bay development project, Cardiff Waterfront first came to prominence as Wales' economic and commercial hub when coal was king and Wales was at the very centre of the industry worldwide.

Elizabethan and Jacobean historical styles. Businessmen were treated to decorative plasterwork ceilings, elaborate fireplaces and two clocks held by statues of lions showing the high tides of Cardiff. It is said that in its heyday up to ten thousand people a day would enter the building. As you'd expect in a late Victorian building constructed with no expense spared, the detailing is highly decorative. A stained glass window of stylised ships contains the inscription 'Ye Olde Order Changeth', and it was this building that enabled such change.

After 1910, Barry took over as the largest volume export dock for coal, with its more modern docks that were less influenced by the tides. Exports fell through the inter-war years and the industry never recovered after World War II. The visitor today may read new meaning into the inscription in that window, as, at the time of writing, the Coal Exchange is in a sorry state of repair, and its future uncertain.

Alterations in the 1970s have done the building no favours: the underground car park mars the main entrance court, and a false ceiling disfigures the main trading hall.

The nearby landmark Pierhead Building had fared better and is a successful example of how to find new use for historic structures. Today many first-time visitors to Cardiff Bay assume that it is the Pierhead Building, and not the adjacent Senedd, that houses the Welsh Assembly. That such a mistake could be made is testament to the lasting power of the Marquess of Bute and the architects he employed.

The Pierhead, built in 1896, was designed by the architect William Frame as the offices for the Cardiff Railway Company, successor to the Bute Dock Company. Like the Coal Exchange, it mixes architectural influences, but is generally medieval in style with a French Gothic flavour,

contrasting the classical styled dock offices at Barry. What makes it noticeable is the reddish glow of the glazed terracotta bricks produced in north Wales, a strong contrast with the cream and grey stone façades that are the norm in Cardiff. Although built as offices the budget was clearly substantial as the tall clock tower is capped by a crenellated parapet and gargoyles. The exterior is heavily enriched with terracotta ornament including a steam train and ships over the company's motto 'Wrth ddŵr a thân' ('By water and fire'). The interior doesn't disappoint with its decorative rooms, not least the Port Manager's office with castellated and canopied 'medieval' chimneypiece and panelled ceiling.

Following restoration, the building was reopened in 2010 as an education and events centre. The Pierhead is once again significant in the dockscape of Cardiff, and a symbol of the regeneration of Butetown. The reopening of the Pierhead marked the end of two decades of regeneration in the docks creating Cardiff Bay. The capital remodelled the bay area with huge investment and a drive to bring people to the waterfront area to live, shop and eat. It was largely successful, helped particularly by the location of the new Senedd on the waterfront. It could be said that some areas of the Cardiff Bay project haven't worked as well as others, but the overall transformation is to be commended.

It is fitting that as devolution brought more power to Wales it turned to its dockland to redevelop as the face of the new Wales. These were the streets and buildings that had made Wales great. This

time Wales wasn't selling its resources, it was remodelling the bay to tell the world that Cardiff was again booming, and was ready to take its place once more alongside the great cities of the world.

Above: Cardiff Coal Exchange Trading Floor in 1912, on its opening after renovation. It is said that in its heyday some ten thousand people a day entered the building.

Left: Cardiff Coal Exchange.

The Wales Millennium Centre is undoubtedly the most successful, and popular of the millennial construction work on Cardiff Waterfront. Built to a striking design by Jonathan Adams of Percy Thomas architects, it has become the most recognisable and loved building in the area.

The Millennium Centre is the premier theatre and arts venue in Wales, and replaces the earlier project to build the Cardiff Bay Opera House to a remarkable design by Zaha Hadid. At the time many were furious that this was rejected, but as time has passed people have grown to love the more practical project by Adams.

The bronzed steel 'armadillo' dome of the Wales Millennium Centre is punctured with lines by poet Gwyneth Lewis, and is probably the most popular Cardiff construction of the last few decades.

Toll Cottage and Cob

Porthmadog, the Cob, the planned town of Tremadog and the Ffestiniog Railway represent Wales' great industrial past, built upon trade and commerce

The Cob at Porthmadog

The Toll Cottage

Porthmadog was by no means a backwater during the late eighteenth century. It was made famous by William Madocks who had created a model town, Tremadog, on an area of barren marsh. The new port exported slate all over the world following the building of the Cob, a sea wall crossing Traeth Mawr from Ynys Towyn in Caernarfonshire to Penrhyn Point in Meirionethshire, between 1808 and 1811. The massive stone-lined barrier was 1,600 yards in length, 90 feet in width at its base and 18 feet high. It cost the Madocks family around £60,000 to complete after rough storms caused it to require extensive repairs in its early years. The development of ports for import and export grew in conjunction with the improvement of roads, and the opening up of Wales. Turnpikes enabled communication between the more remote regions of Britain with London, and this no doubt hastened the transference of ideas more easily. These roads created an integral infrastructure for turning what were once distant and isolated areas into new territory for expansion, territory which, to William Madocks, included Porthmadog.

William Madocks lived at a cottage in Tan-yr-Allt, above Tremadog, which he bought in 1798.

Toll Cottage and Cob

People: William Madocks, owner; Captain Joseph Huddart, entrepreneur (1741-1816).

Place: Madocks' project, to create 1,500 acres of new land and a seaport, was enabled by building the Cob, an artificial embankment over which the road and rail run.

Event: Porthmadog, the Cob, the planned town of Tremadog and the Ffestiniog Railway represent Wales' great industrial past, built on trade and commerce.

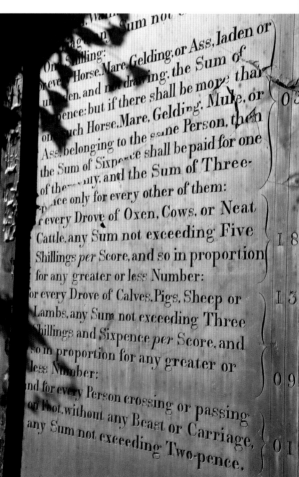

Madocks presumably bought the existing house for its views, and soon built around it a pattern-book regency villa circa 1800. Tan-yr-Allt is believed to be one of the first villas to be built in Wales, and it was much copied as the picturesque movement swept through Wales. The house was described by Percy Bysshe Shelley as a 'cottage extensive and tasty enough for the villa of an Italian prince'. Shelley found life in north-west Wales quite difficult, referring to the local society as 'very stupid. They are all aristocrats and saints. The unpleasant part of the business is, that they hunt people to death, who are not so likewise'.

Following parliamentary approval in 1807 Madocks reclaimed land at Traeth Mawr from the original estuary of Afon Glaslyn with the building of the Cob, creating 1,500 acres of new land. He had initially envisaged using the newly formed harbour as the start of a shipping route to Ireland, and hydrographer Captain Joseph Huddart was called to survey coastal towns for the most suitable route for

running the mail packet across the Irish Sea. Porthmadog was championed by Madocks but Holyhead was finally chosen instead, a decision which caused no small financial hardship for the Madocks family. Huddart, however, fell in love with the area and, in 1809, purchased part of the historic Brynkir estate in Cwm Pennant. The Madocks and Huddart families played a major role in the Industrial Revolution in this part of Wales, investing in the Ffestiniog Railway and numerous quarrying and mining ventures, including largely unsuccessful ones in and near Cwm Pennant. The Ffestiniog Railway used the Cob to transport slate from the Blaenau Ffestiniog quarries to Porthmadog for export. The line was upgraded to a narrow gauge railway in 1863, closing in 1946, but was reopened in 1955. It still operates to this day as a Trust and is a major tourist attraction in north-west Wales.

Porthmadog, the Cob, the planned town of Tremadog and the Ffestiniog Railway represent Wales' great industrial past,

built upon trade and commerce. Slate had been its major catalyst, but the building of a port enabled the creation of new communities, dependent on the work provided by the quarries, and also tourism. The Llyn Peninsula became accessible for the general public, who came for holidays at Pwllheli and Abersoch by train or sea. Madocks' vision cannot be underestimated, for if he had not been expansive in his approach, much we now love about north-west Wales would be either inaccessible or just another man's dream.

The Ffestiniog Railway used the Cob to transport slate from the Blaenau Ffestiniog quarries to Porthmadog for export

Big Pit,
Blaenavon

The new industries caused large-scale immigration and urbanisation, fundamentally reordering Welsh society, religion and economy

Big Pit, Blaenavon

People: The population of south Wales.

Place: Big Pit, Blaenavon. UNESCO World Heritage Site and National Museum Wales' industrial heritage site showcasing the coal industry.

Event: Coal was the catalyst for change in the south during the nineteenth century with industrialisation, immigration and urbanisation transforming Welsh society from its agricultural past to a modern industrial nation.

Slate and copper were the boom industries of north Wales, while iron, steel and coal, also known as black gold, were by far the biggest sources of fortune and employment in the south. In fact, coal-mining was to dominate Wales for nearly two hundred years before its eventual rapid decline at the end of the twentieth century. The impact of the income from the coal industry cannot therefore be underestimated in terms of the urban expansion of the towns and cities of south Wales, as well as upon the building and furnishing of the country houses of the region. For the duration of the nineteenth century, many south Wales gentry families, such as the Butes of Cardiff Castle and the Morgans of Tredegar, were sustained by the wealth brought in by

coal. The new industries caused large-scale immigration and urbanisation, fundamentally reordering Welsh society, religion and economy. There was a simultaneous rise in political radicalism, something which helped shape a new Welsh identity away from its agricultural origins.

The coal pits of south Wales peppered the valleys. Mining villages and towns thrived in the shadow of the mines, with schools, working men's clubs, chapels, shops and a proud sense of community. Big Pit at Blaenavon is National Museum Wales' industrial heritage site showcasing the coal industry, with evidence of mining in the Blaenavon area going back to the fourteenth century. Big Pit functioned as a working pit between 1860 and 1980,

employing nearly 1500 people at its peak in the 1920s. It was purchased by the National Museum in 1980 and was opened to the public three years later. Big Pit is only one of two remaining mines where it is possible to travel beneath the earth's surface to the working coal face, with, in this case, the original miners' cages being used to transport visitors down to the depths of the mine some 300 feet below. The pit, together with the nearby town of Blaenavon, is part of a UNESCO World Heritage Site which also includes the Blaenavon Ironworks, Pontypool and Blaenavon Railway and the Blaenavon World Heritage Centre. Wales' industrial past is truly preserved in this illustrious town. One of the features of Blaenavon which places it on an

international stage is the world's first railway viaduct, built in 1790 for horse-drawn carts to carry coal from the mines.

Mining provided significant sources of money for Wales throughout the nineteenth and early twentieth centuries, with Wales leading the rest of Britain into the Industrial Revolution. The South Wales Coalfield stretches from Pembrokeshire in the west to Caerphilly County in the east, with the docks at Cardiff, then later at Barry, being the largest coal exporting ports. The world's first one million pound business deal was transacted at Cardiff's Coal Exchange in 1907, highlighting the immense amount of money that was entering Wales at its industrial peak.

The world's first one million pound business deal was transacted at Cardiff's Coal Exchange in 1907

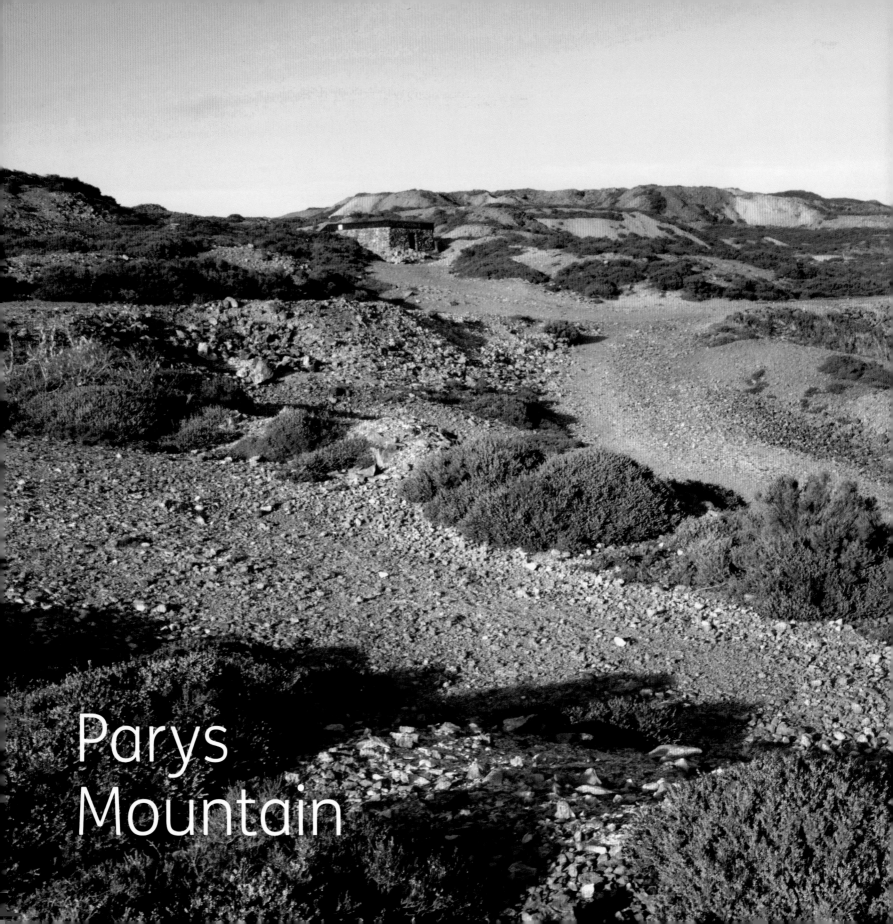

Parys
Mountain

The story of one of Wales' richest families began with an heiress who inherited a barren hillside on the Llys Dulas estate

Parys Mountain

People: Mary Lewis (1740-1835), heiress of the Chancellor of Bangor Cathedral and wife of Rev. Edward Hughes (1739-1815) .

Place: Parys Mountain, Anglesey. A barren patch of land which, in 1768, was found to be immensely rich in copper and became one of Britain's largest open cast copper mines serving the entire British Empire.

Event: Parys Mountain dominated the world's copper market during the 1780s when the mine was the largest in Europe. Its copper was used by the British Admiralty to protect wooden ships, allowing them to remain at sea for longer.

Mary Lewis

The Reverend Edward Hughes

Copper was the fortune of Parys Mountain, one of Wales' greatest export items of the eighteenth century.

The story of one of Wales' richest families began with an heiress who inherited a barren hillside on the Llys Dulas estate. The Hugheses of Lleiniog were an old Anglesey family who claimed descent from Hwfa ap Cynddelw, possessor of the Lordship of Llysllifon and founder of the first of the fifteen Noble Tribes of Wales. It was through Mary Lewis that the Llys Dulas estate entered the Hughes family's hands. For Mary's inheritance included a portion of Parys Mountain, an area of Anglesey which was found to be immensely rich in copper and which provided the Hughes family with a vast, if sudden, income.

The Hughes dynasty was founded by Hugh Hughes (1705-1773) who, in 1725, had entered the employ of Dr. Edward Wynn of Bodewryd, Chancellor of Hereford. Hugh rose from servant to landowner during the mid-eighteenth century, acquiring the Lleiniog estate near Beaumaris. His son, Rev. Edward Hughes married Mary Lewis of Llys Dulas in 1765, shortly before the 'great lode' of copper ore was discovered at Parys Mountain on 2nd March 1768. With their new found fortune, the Hugheses spent lavishly on acquiring property, purchasing the Kinmel Estate in 1786 for £42,000 which then became the principal residence of the family.

Parys Mountain grew from a relatively modest enterprise to open-cast and then, finally, as the copper was found deeper,

with adits and shafts. The ore was broken into small pieces by hand and then shipped to Swansea and Lancashire for smelting. Welsh copper dominated the world's market during the 1780s with uses including protecting the bottom of British Admiralty vessels against the actions of the teredo worm, a clam with a worm-like body, which bored into ships' hulls. At its peak the profits were £300,000 per year, a sum which was split with the Hughes' co-owners, the Baylys of Plas Newydd, Anglesey. Between 1768 and 1904, around 3.5 million tonnes of ore was removed from Parys Mountain, irrevocably changing the natural landscape. The chemical by-products were made famous by Augustin Gottfried Ludwig Lentin (1764-1823) who

Left: Mary Lewis, heiress of Llys Dulas, married her father's employee, Edward Hughes, curate to Robert Lewis, Rector of Trefdraeth and Chancellor of Bangor Cathedral. Edward Hughes' business negotiations on behalf of his wife and her inheritance, caused Mr. and Mrs. Hughes to become one of the richest couples in late-eighteenth century Wales.

visited Parys Mountain in the 1790s. His publication detailed the sulphur, vitriol, alum and ochre pigments that were also being produced.

Today, the toxicity of the site is so high that little life can survive on or near the mountain. It appears as an alien landscape, so very different to the rest of Anglesey. The 1997 movie *Mortal Kombat Annihilation* was partially filmed there and the location is often used for photo and film shoots. The site still contains large resources of copper, lead and zinc totalling nearly 6,500,000 tonnes and there are hopes of continuing the tradition of mining on the mountain.

Parys Mountain grew from a relatively modest enterprise, to open-cast, and then finally, as the copper was found deeper, with adits and shafts

Tredegar Central Surgery

The principle behind the Medical Aid Society at Tredegar has influenced modern Britain and our expectation of free health care for all

Tredegar Central Surgery

People: Aneurin Bevan (1897-1960), Labour Minister for Health 1945-1951.

Place: 10 The Circle, Tredegar, home of the Medical Aid Society. Central Surgery, founded by the society in 1911.

Event: Tredegar-born Aneurin Bevan was so influenced by the healthcare provided in his hometown by the Medical Aid Society that he used it as the template for building the modern NHS.

Some people in Wales won't know Tredegar Central Surgery, and wouldn't realise why it is a structure significant in building modern Wales and Britain. Yet this humble Edwardian redbrick has influenced the world. Once we remind people that Aneurin Bevan was born in Tredegar they will understand the significance of the building. Bevan, the Labour politician, is regarded as one of the leading parliamentarians and orators of the twentieth century, and a key architect in establishing the National Health Service. That service was modelled by Bevan on the Medical Aid society based at Tredegar Central Surgery, and we can trace the principles of modern day health care to this small Monmouthshire society.

The National Health Service has gone on to influence countless other healthcare systems around the world.

The Medical Aid Society in Tredegar started out in the ordinary terraced buildings at 10 The Circle. It was there that the concept for the Society was thought up and first implemented, and the group built the Tredegar cottage hospital in 1904. By 1911 they'd opened the red-brick Central Surgery that is the building most people think of today when they refer to the good work of the Society. The surgery provided medical care for the people of Tredegar and was funded by a percentage subscription from the wages of the workers of the town. The

attractive building has a mildly Arts and Crafts feel, mixing terracotta and Bath-stone with arches and scrolls. It was home to a pharmacy, consultancy and treatment rooms on the ground floor and accommodation for two doctors and their families upstairs. We're unsure who the architect was, but it may have been E. A. Johnson of Abergavenny who already had a relationship with the Society, having designed the cottage hospital.

The principle behind the Medical Aid Society in Tredegar was simple: for a small weekly donation out of wages, workmen would receive medical care when required without further payment. The Society wasn't the first or the largest in Wales (there were several similar systems established by groups of workers in the Monmouthshire valleys), but it was one of the most sophisticated and comprehensive in its cover. It is notable for having provided medical benefit to the entire community, and not just to those workers who contributed to the scheme. In the Medical Aid Society the people of Tredegar created what would become the model for the 1948 National Health Service.

The root of societies like Tredegar go as far back as the early industrialisation of Wales when the developing iron industry deducted a payment from the wage packet in return for paying surgeons to care for workers and their families. As the nineteenth century developed, and the iron industries were replaced by steel and coal, groups of workers acted to take control of these early health schemes, so that the workers rather than the employers were controlling the system. Some employers had been profiting from the medical payments and others, more benign, were subsidising them.

In Tredegar the Medical Aid scheme was initially confined to those employed by the Tredegar Iron and Coal Company but soon expanded to include the family members of those who contributed, local workers, shopkeepers and teachers, and eventually gave aid to all who required it. Miners and steelworkers paid a weekly subscription of twopence in each pound of their wages while 'town subscribers' were required to pay 18 shillings a year. For an extra fourpence a week, members were covered for hospital treatment. By the 1940s, when it was used by Bevan as the model for his National system, the Society provided medical care for 22,800 of the town's 24,000 inhabitants.

Bevan was born and raised in Tredegar, and worked as miner for the Tredegar Iron and Coal Company, so he knew the Medical Aid Society well. He also served on the Tredegar Hospital Management Committee. After being elected to Parliament for Ebbw Vale, which includes Tredegar, he was appointed Minister for Health in Clement Attlee's 1945 government. In 1946 the medical aid societies of south Wales met with Bevan and he recorded their influence on him: 'I know the valuable services rendered by Associations. I have been closely associated with them for many years, even from boyhood.'

The NHS took from Tredegar the concept of universality; the Tredegar society helped all, including the unemployed. Contributors paid a percentage of their income rather than a set fee, so the wealthy contributed more than the poor. Bevan ensured that eligibility for healthcare covered every citizen and that all contributed according to their means and benefited according to their needs, not according to their ability to pay. As Bevan commented: 'The essence of a satisfactory health service is that the rich and the poor are treated alike, that poverty is not a disability, and wealth is not advantaged.'

The National Health Service was established in July 1948, though Bevan resigned from the government in 1951 when NHS charges were introduced on false teeth and glasses. The Medical Aid Society was made defunct by its success in inspiring a National System, and today the building has an appropriate new use as a care home.

The principle behind the Medical Aid

Aneurin Bevan addresses a crowd.

Society at Tredegar has influenced modern Britain and our expectation of free health care for all. We only have to look over the water to the United States of America to see how, a century later, other countries have failed to care adequately for the sick. Wales should be proud of its role in establishing the NHS and also of its tradition of working-class radicalism born from Welsh industry. The same Welsh spirit that inspired Tredegar led David Lloyd George to introduce old age pension payments in 1909. We owe that generation a great deal, and we should fight to preserve the good work they undertook.

'I know the valuable services rendered by Associations. I have been closely associated with them for many years, even from boyhood'
Aneurin Bevan

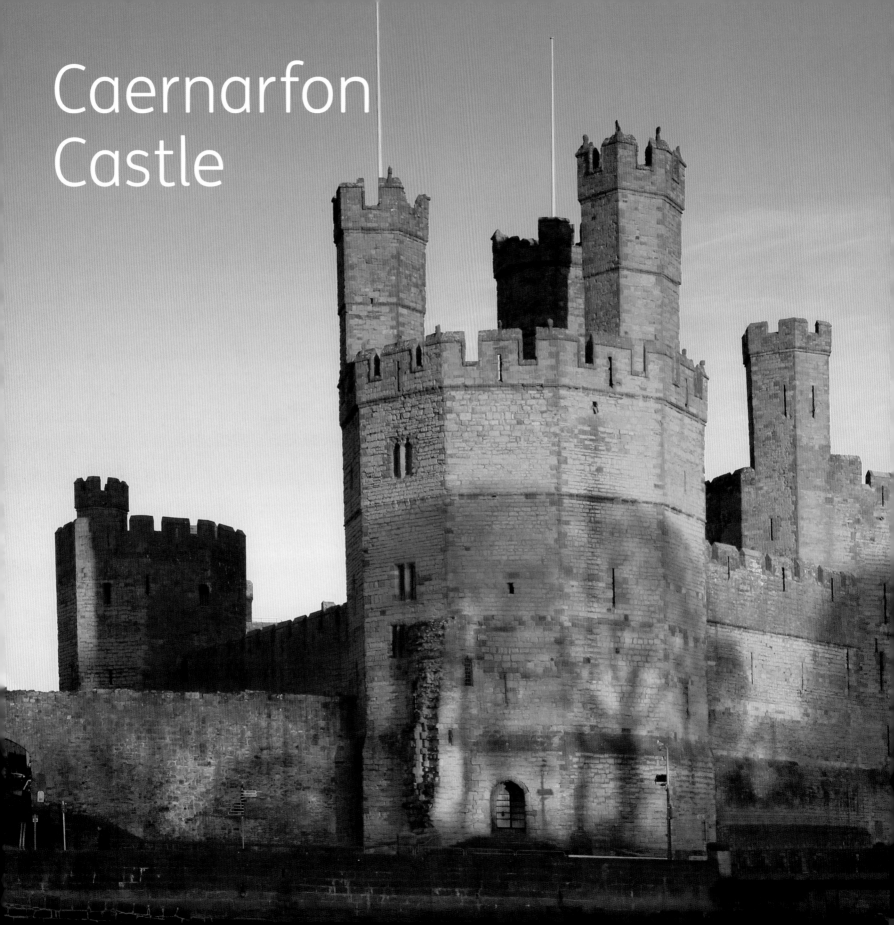

Caernarfon Castle

Caernarfon Castle

People: Edward I; Llywelyn ap Gruffydd

Place: Alongside Harlech, Conwy and Beaumaris, Caernarfon Castle is one of a series of stone castles built by Edward I in the thirteenth century to suppress the native Welsh population. Now a World Heritage Site in the care of Cadw.

Event: Following the rebellion of Llywelyn ap Gruffydd, Edward I determined that the way to subdue a hostile population was through a show of military strength. Caernarfon Castle became Edward's 'capital' in north Wales from where he was able to colonise and settle the region under his rule.

Caernarfon Castle is iconic. It represents so many different things to many different people. For some, it is the oppression of the Welsh by a conquering force; for others, the expression of medieval architectural mastery and an attempt to assimilate royal authority over a local population. Whatever the view, it cannot be denied that the castle is magnificent and has become a major world-renowned tourist attraction.

Since prehistoric times the area around Caernarfon has proved beneficial for human inhabitation. The shores of the Menai Strait and the rich natural resources of the area enabled the Romans to found the fort of Segontium in AD80. It became the most important military base and administrative centre in Roman north-west Wales, surviving until the fall of Rome.

Llywelyn ap Gruffydd's refusal to pay homage to Edward I led to the thirteenth-century conquest of Wales by the English king. From 1277, and particularly after 1283, Edward embarked on a policy of English colonisation and settlement of Wales, determining that military security would be paramount in subduing a hostile population. Edward's castle at Caernarfon was one of a series of stone fortresses designed to form a ring of stone around north Wales; indeed Caernarfon Castle was eventually to become one of the largest of the English castles ever built in Wales. The borough of Caernarfon was constituted in 1284 under the terms of the Statute of Rhuddlan, but the castle was actually started a year earlier, in 1283, as the motte and bailey structure which had stood there previously began to be replaced. Eventually, in 1330,

The grandiose construction is breath-taking, symbolising medieval architectural achievement on one hand, and Welsh suppression on the other

with many of the interior buildings still unfinished, work came to an end, with the total cost at this point estimated to have been between £20,000 and £25,000.

The town walls encircled the newly established town, and a dock was created for import and export. Edward I and his wife, Eleanor, visited in 1283 and stayed for just over a month whilst the foundations were being laid. They returned again in 1284 to view the progression of works, staying in specially erected timber apartments. Legend states that Edward I had promised the Welsh that they would have a ruler who was born in Wales and would be fluent in his native tongue. It was during this second visit that Edward II was born at Caernarfon, and was made the first Prince of Wales in 1301.

As the wars subsided and the Tudor dynasty settled political affairs, the need for castles diminished. The royal apartments were still available for state visits but, by and large, they were derelict by the seventeenth century. During the Civil War, Caernarfon was garrisoned by Royalists and was besieged three times by Parliamentarians, finally surrendering in 1646. In 1660, the castle was decommissioned and became a romantic ruin, much loved by the followers of the Picturesque.

In 1911, Caernarfon came to national prominence once again when it was used for the Investiture of the Prince of Wales, later the ill-fated Edward VIII. He was crowned within the castle walls by his father, George V. The ceremony was masterminded by David Lloyd George, Liberal leader and son of the county, who wanted the Prince to champion the Welsh cause. The Investiture was a glitzy affair and mesmerised those who attended. The young Prince was presented to the nation from a balcony, built at the original entrance into the castle complex. It echoed the medieval pomp and pageantry much admired by Lloyd George and his view of nationhood. With a precedent set, Charles, Prince of Wales, was invested at Caernarfon in a televised ceremony in 1969; though not without controversy it has to be said.

Caernarfon Castle is now in the care of Cadw, and was added to UNESCO's list of World Heritage Sites in 1986. The grandiose construction is truly breath-taking, symbolising medieval architectural achievement on one hand and the suppression of an indigenous population on the other.

Caernarfon Castle was eventually to become one of the largest of the English castles ever built in Wales

Capel Celyn, Tryweryn

The buildings of Capel Celyn are not visible to the eye today, and yet they stand strong in the national consciousness of Wales

Capel Celyn, Tryweryn

People: The villagers of Capel Celyn; the Palace of Westminster and Liverpool City Council.

Place: Capel Celyn, previously home to 67 people and now submerged under the Tryweryn River. A site of great significance to the nationalist movement.

Event: In 1957 Liverpool City Council needed water for its growing population. To avoid Welsh consultation, the plan to create a new reservoir at Capel Celyn went before Parliament, with the result that the village was submerged despite almost universal Welsh opposition.

If you Google the location of the north Wales village of Capel Celyn you may be surprised by the result. The familiar red Google marker appears to point to the middle of an expanse of water about a mile wide and two and a half miles long, between Trawsfynydd and Bala in Gwynedd. Google hasn't made an error: their marker is in a correct position. This place has become known as Tryweryn after the river that flows down the valley. Capel Celyn and its community have been replaced by that river, infamously drowned in the early 1960s to provide a reservoir of water for Liverpool.

The buildings of Capel Celyn are not visible to the eye today, and yet they stand strong in the national consciousness of Wales. Sometimes, in a year of severe draught, their remains become clearly visible in the mud and people come on

Protests before the valley was flooded.

After years of protest during the dam construction the valley was finally flooded in 1965, and the Tryweryn reservoir opened.

pilgrimage. You'll notice people taking photographs, sitting quietly and feeling the anger and the sense of loss that still resonates there. These were always unremarkable buildings, and today they are mostly demolished, but they are felt even when they cannot be seen. You'll see them represented in Welsh art, and you'll hear them referred to in Welsh songs.

Tryweryn has become a single word that recalls the insensitivity of English corporations and Government in their relationships with Welsh culture and communities. Despite universal condemnation and outrage within Wales, the community at Capel Celyn was obliterated by the flooding of their valley to create the Tryweryn reservoir in the early 1960s. The voice of Wales was loud in her objection. The dam was bombed. Politicians, activists, ordinary people all spoke out and resisted the flooding of the valley of Capel Celyn. Despite the outrage, the valley was still flooded, a community

was lost, and Wales will probably never forget the pain of that wound. Yet out of that sadness and anger grew a strengthened Welsh nationalism, and today the word Tryweryn has become a symbol to embolden the heart of anyone reminded of the inequalities put upon Wales.

The small community of Capel Celyn was drowned under a 1957 Act of Parliament that had been brought to Westminster by Liverpool City Council. The very system by which permission was obtained caused anger, as by applying for an Act of Parliament via a private bill, Liverpool avoided the necessity of acquiring planning consent from the Welsh authorities. They knew this, and the fact that all Welsh MPs at the time voted against the bill was evidence enough of feeling within Wales about the project. It was a clear demonstration that Wales was entirely powerless against decisions made in London.

Some 48 out of 67 people resident around Capel Celyn lost their homes when the new reservoir was created. It was a strong community known for its rich Welsh language culture and, to many in Wales, the drowning of the valley felt like an attack on Welsh-speaking Wales. The buildings at Capel Celyn were not significant in architectural terms. Although one of the farms, Hafod Fadog, was a noted early Quaker meeting place and cemetery, the significance of this place was simply that it was typical. Drowned were the farms, the houses, the village school, the Post Office. These were ordinary stone buildings, but the structure which created the community of Capel Celyn.

The fact that the chapel with its cemetery was also destroyed was particularly offensive to the people of Capel Celyn and rural Wales. These days many chapels have fallen empty, been converted, or even demolished, but in

The valley of Capel Celyn before it was flooded.

the early 1960s the flooding of a chapel showed a significant disregard of rural Welsh sensibilities. Some of the stones from that chapel have been used in the construction of the replacement Memorial Chapel, which remains a site of pilgrimage to this day. The families were given the option of having the bodies from the cemetery disinterred and moved to another cemetery. Eight were, and the remainder were capped in concrete and flooded along with the world that they represented. Gravestones were all moved up to the new chapel as markers of what had been lost.

The language of Capel Celyn was Welsh, and this is reflected in the names of the farms and houses that have been lost. Gone are Coed Mynach, Garnedd Lwyd,

and Bryn Hyfryd; drowned are Gelli Uchaf, Penbryn Mawr and Tŷ Nant among others. An ordinary, and yet pristine community was ripped from its natural surroundings against its will. Had the purpose been to provide essential drinking water for the area, or even for Wales, the insult may have been easier to bear.

After years of protest during the dam construction the valley was finally flooded in 1965, and the Tryweryn reservoir (now Llyn Celyn) opened, providing water for Liverpool City and the Wirral. Despite bombings at the dam construction site by Mudiad Amddiffyn Cymru (MAC), the project was completed and the residents of Capel Celyn were forced from their homes. Most of the buildings were at least partially demolished before the rising

reservoir reached them, but in drought years their traces can still be seen as ghostly reminders of the insensitivity of Westminster. The official opening ceremony in October 1965 saw huge protests, and lasted a mere three minutes as protesters succeeded in cutting the wires to the loudspeakers so that nothing could be heard over the shouting.

The lasting effect of the destruction of Capel Celyn was an increased appetite for Welsh devolution. Plaid Cymru saw increased support because of the Tryweryn protest and the fact that all Welsh MPs objected to the proposal yet could change nothing. In England there were also many who objected to the flooding of an occupied valley. It is difficult to tie change specifically to the

'Cofiwch Dryweryn' Remember Tryweryn.

Tryweryn protest, but it was also in 1957 that the Council of Wales recommended that Wales get her own Secretary of State and that a Welsh Office be created. The 1964 Harold Wilson government granted these changes and, in the year after the reservoir opening, Gwynfor Evans won Plaid's first Westminster seat in Carmarthen against a background of raised national consciousness.

Forty years after the flooding, on 19 October 2005, Liverpool City Council formally apologised for the flooding at Capel Celyn:

'The Council acknowledges its debt to the many thousands of Welsh people who have made their homes in the City. They have, in so many ways, enriched the life of the City....We realise the hurt of forty years ago when the Tryweryn Valley was transformed into a reservoir to help meet the water needs of Liverpool.

For any insensitivity by our predecessor Council at that time, we apologise and hope that the historic and sound relationship between Liverpool and Wales can be completely restored.'

As you drive down the A487 coast road south from Aberystwyth today, you'll be reminded by graffiti to 'Cofiwch Dryweryn' as you approach Llanrhystud. It's a famous piece of protest art that has been regularly repainted over the decades. The people of Wales probably don't need to 'Remember Tryweryn' as the history of a once unassuming village has become emblematic to many of something much greater: the insensitive way in which the UK government once trampled over the culture and values of part of its indigenous population.

Forty years after the flooding, on 19 October 2005, Liverpool City Council formally apologised for the flooding at Capel Celyn

'Parliament'
of Glyndŵr

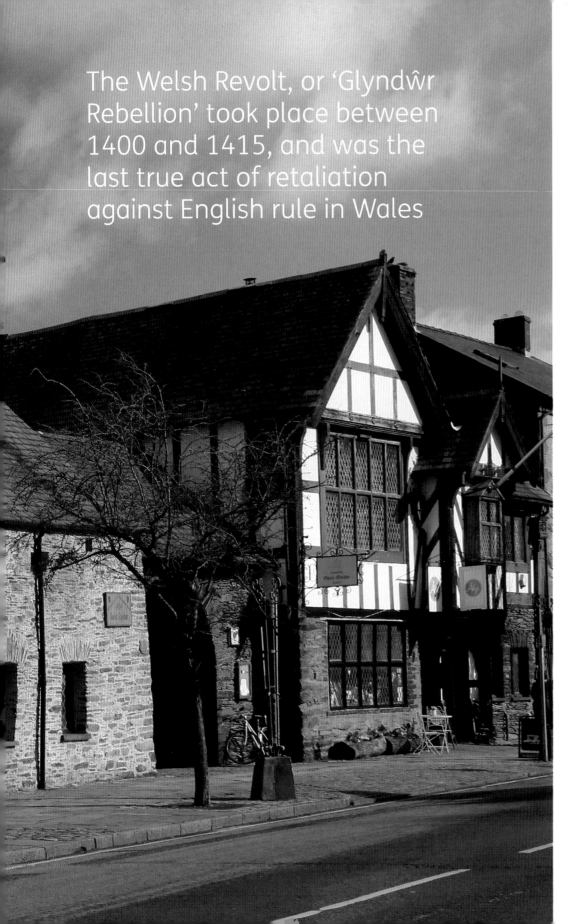

The Welsh Revolt, or 'Glyndŵr Rebellion' took place between 1400 and 1415, and was the last true act of retaliation against English rule in Wales

'Parliament' of Glyndŵr

People: Owain Glyndŵr

Place: Parliament House, Machynlleth, the reputed site of Owain Glyndŵr's parliament held in 1404. The building was given to the town of Machynlleth by David Davies, later Lord of Llandinam, in 1912 and is now home to a National Heritage Centre.

Event: In 1404, at the height of his rebellion against the English, Owain Glyndŵr was crowned Prince of Wales and held what was to be the last parliament in Wales for nearly 600 years.

Owain Glyndŵr is an almost mythical hero from Welsh history, whose legacy is both inspiring yet controversial. Glyndŵr was the last native Prince of Wales and his wars against the English King, Henry IV, have gone down in legend as the last stand against Wales' loss of independence. The Welsh Revolt or 'Glyndŵr Rebellion' took place between 1400 and 1415, and was the last true act of retaliation against English rule in Wales.

Owain Glyndŵr was born in north-east Wales into an Anglo-Welsh gentry family. On both sides, he was descended from pre-Conquest Welsh gentry and, due to

his kinship links with the Marcher Lords, was sent to London to study law. He joined the English crown's military ranks and fought alongside the great names of late thirteenth-century England. During the 1390s, Glyndŵr returned to his Welsh estates and all was well until the Baron Grey de Ruthyn took Glyndŵr's lands. An appeal to the English Parliament fell on deaf ears and Baron Grey played foul with the ensuing legal case. Civil unrest broke out in Chester following the execution of one of the late Richard II's supporters. Glyndŵr assumed his family's ancestral title of Prince of Powys and, with a small

band of followers, laid siege to Baron Grey's lands.

The revolt spread over much of north and mid Wales in 1401 and, in 1402, Glyndŵr captured Baron Grey and sold him back to the English for a great ransom. Glyndŵr won many battles. The French and Bretons offered their support to the fight against the English monarchy, as they had done with the Scots. In 1403, the whole of Wales became embroiled in the revolt, with countrymen returning to wage war against the English. Glyndŵr was strong enough to call his first Parliament of Wales at Machynlleth in 1404, where

he was crowned Prince of Wales and set out his political agenda for his principality. Wales was to be an independent state, with a separate parliament and church; the Laws of Hywel Dda would return and two national universities would be founded, one in the north and one in the south.

Machynlleth was chosen due to its central location and for its situation within Powys. Parliament House is a hall house, and the Royal Commission's tree ring dating has found that some of its timbers date back to 1470. This may be nearly seventy years later than the parliament itself, but it does suggest that the site has early origins. The Royal Commission dendrochronology project began in 1996. It has shown that surviving late-medieval houses date post-1400, after the Owain Glyndŵr rebellion, and that there was a great late-medieval rebuilding, but that it was socially and chronologically staggered. Post-1400 architecture in Wales developed very

differently to that of England, Scotland and Ireland; the Welsh house was often undefended and associated more with entertainment and hospitality than strength and security. Hall building and design developed into a high craft; one which was praised by bardic poetry and used by all strata of medieval society in Wales. The most common building type was the three unit plan: open hall, set between storeyed upper and lower bays with chambers. Timber was the main material used for construction; full crucks being used in north and east Wales whilst jointed/scarfed crucks were favoured in south and west Wales.

Lord Davies of Llandinam gave the Parliament House to the town of Machynlleth in 1912, having purchased it in 1906. Davies wanted to preserve a symbolic moment in Welsh history. The site has been long associated with the parliament. It is also a rare survivor of a late-medieval Welsh town house

and therefore unusual and to be valued. Davies spent lavishly restoring the old house, and built the Owain Glyndŵr Institute next door. Probably designed by Frank Shayler of Shrewsbury, an architect favoured by Davies, the Institute was a sympathetic Tudor revival affair. One of the most famous features of the interior of Parliament House is Murray Urquhart's mural depicting scenes from Glyndŵr's life, particularly the battle of Hyddgen. The mural took Urquhart two years to complete and was unveiled in 1914.

It has taken nearly six hundred years for Glyndŵr's aspirations to take form. His vision of Wales as its own distinct entity has been given significant boosts during the twentieth and twenty-first centuries. His legacy and evocative story are preserved in the writings of historians and the visitor experience to Parliament House. The buildings are also testament to the life of Lord Davies, whose generosity in the early-twentieth century saved the building from any potentially inappropriate development. It did dishearten many when the date of the Parliament House was set to 1470, but it does not diminish the symbolic nature of Glyndŵr's cause and his desire for Wales to better itself intrinsically. It may not have been the actual parliament building but it has come to embody all that it stands for – Owain Glyndŵr and his consolidation of a nation.

Cathays Park

Cathays Park

People: John Crichton-Stuart, Third Marquess of Bute (1847-1900).

Place: A collection of buildings including Cardiff City Hall (opened 1906), the National Museum (1913-27), Cardiff Crown Court (1904) and the Glamorgan Building (1909-11).

Event: In 1898 Lord Bute sold 59 acres of land to Cardiff on condition that they were used for 'civic, cultural and educational' purposes. The result is the Civic Centre of Cathays Park, the 'finest civic centre in the British Isles'.

The buildings and layout of Cardiff's elegant Cathays Park have often been described as the finest Edwardian civic architecture in Britain, and are worthy of inclusion in this book for this reason. Yet they also give a sense of nationhood to Wales in their grandeur: despite being built well before Cardiff became the capital of Wales in 1955.

Today it seems natural that the 'National' buildings of Cathays Park were built for a capital city. Yet they were planned and constructed around half a century before

Cardiff was granted this status. Cardiff was little more than a small county town until the early nineteenth century, with a population of just 1,870 in the 1801 census, making it the 25th largest town in Wales. It would be a further century before it was given city status in 1905. For years Merthyr Tydfil was considered to be Wales' major town, with Swansea another contender.

Left: The Welsh National War Memorial 1924-28 by Sir John Ninian Comper, with a male nude in bronze by Bertram Pegram.

Above: Cathays Park is laid out around handsome wide avenues.

The development of the docks in the mid-nineteenth century radically changed Cardiff's economy and today, if you include the wider metropolitan area, the capital is home to over a third of Wales' three million inhabitants. Even so, for a capital it remains on a human scale with a layout and centre that is easy to navigate. Like all great cities Cardiff has several fine parks, and the formal gardens and buildings of Cathays Park are an asset to the nation.

Cathays Park is home to a wonderful collection of early twentieth-century buildings: notably Cardiff City Hall, the National Museum, Cardiff Crown Court and the Glamorgan Building, though there is interest too in the smaller structures including the restrained 'Deco' feeling of the Temple of Peace (1937-8) by Sir Percy Thomas and the Welsh National War

Memorial (1924-28) by Sir John Ninian Comper, with a male nude in Bronze by Betram Pegram. The Pevsner guide for Glamorgan describes Cathays Park as the 'finest civic centre in the British Isles' and they are not wrong; perfect planning and proportion has left Wales with a variety of first-rate early twentieth-century buildings in dramatically different styles that are united by their use of Portland stone. Together these structures form something greater than the sum of their parts and have helped build our sense of nationhood.

As with so much of Cardiff, the story of Cathays Park begins with the Marquesses of Bute, and particularly the third Marquess who sold fifty-nine acres to the town council for £160,000 in 1898 on condition that they developed the land for 'civic, cultural and educational'

purposes, and that the existing avenues were to be preserved. William Harpur is responsible for the excellent civil planning; at Cathays Park we can see that it is often the spaces between buildings as much as the buildings themselves that create the architectural harmony. One of the many statues in the park is of the third Marquess, John Crichton-Stuart, who stands among topiary in Friary Gardens. Today the 'Park' is a collection of public and University buildings around a formal garden centred on the attractive Welsh National War Memorial.

The first two buildings were the Law courts and Town (now City) Hall constructed 1901-1904 to a design of Lanchester, Stewart & Rickards. This grand pair are in a neo-Baroque style, with allegorical figurative decoration of Commerce and Industry and Science and

Education on the Crown Court, and Unity and Patriotism and Poetry and Music on the City Hall. The particularly sumptuous and original interior of City Hall contains a collection of statues of Welsh heroes (1912-1917) financed by D. A. Thomas, Lord Rhondda. It is no surprise that in 1998 many assumed the new Welsh Assembly would be housed in City Hall, which was a ready-made, and available, building of the highest architectural calibre.

It wasn't until 1910, and after Cardiff was awarded city status, that the National Museum of Wales was planned next door, to a design by Smith & Brewer; the National Museum itself having been granted a Royal charter in 1907. It is probably the most handsome of the three, having more controlled and planned decoration that allows the building, rather than the decoration, to 'speak'. Built slightly later than its sisters (1913-27) it differs in style, and has been described as 'American Beaux-Arts' in theme, and compared to the Metropolitan Museum of Art in New York of 1872. The advantage of this particular plot is that the building can run back a long way – perfect for a museum that would inevitably expand over time, as indeed it did in the 1960s and 1990s. Even the original plan was for a building that was twice as deep as it was broad across the front. The First World War interrupted building.

The monumental scale of the three primary buildings, the Courts, City Hall and National Museum, is balanced by formal decorative gardens to the fore and rear. Friary Gardens honours the Marquess of Bute with clipped hedges; Gorsedd Gardens in front of the National Museum is named after the 1899 National Eisteddfod; and Alexandra Gardens was named for Alexandra of Denmark, consort of Edward VII. We shouldn't underestimate the value of these gardens in providing an appropriate setting to display the architecture. The buildings of Cathays Park express Cardiff's claim to being a city of international importance at the peak of its power in the early decades of the twentieth century. The success of the design and architecture is reflected in the fact that it feels like the centre of the nation. That it also retains the tranquillity of a park is quite an achievement.

Dolwyddelan Castle

Dolwyddelan Castle

People: Prince Llywelyn ab Iorwerth (Llywelyn the Great).

Place: Dolwyddelan Castle, one of a series of castles belonging to Welsh princes, now in the care of Cadw.

Event: Reputed birthplace of Llywelyn the Great, Dolwyddelan Castle formed part of the defences of Llywelyn's thirteenth-century mountain kingdom due to its ideal strategic location.

Dolwyddelan holds an evocative place in Welsh history as it is reputed to be the birthplace of Prince Llywelyn ab Iorwerth, Llywelyn the Great. By way of contrast with the conquest fortresses of Edward I's 'ring of stone', the castles of the Welsh princes were far smaller and more compact. Dolwyddelan monitored two routes in Snowdonia and is evidence of Llywelyn the Great's planning of the defence and control of the region. The siting is dramatic, with the tower stark against the skyline and rugged, ripped mountain tops; it could easily be a scene from *Game of Thrones*. As a building it is functional, without ostentation,

and has survived several centuries of being battered by Welsh weather. With a mix of fiscal disadvantage and lack of architectural expertise, the native castles of Wales evince a distinctive style of solidity and pragmatism, making the most of natural vantage points and exploiting local materials.

Dolwyddelan Castle was built of local grit and slate rubble during the early thirteenth century. It consisted of one rectangular tower with two floors. The first floor contained the principal chamber, with an elaborate fireplace and access through a trapdoor to the basement. Dolwyddelan's location placed it within the medieval region of Gwynedd, and it governed an important passing point through Snowdonia. The castle fell to Edward I's forces in 1283. It was altered by the English, who developed the immediate area by constructing a new bridge and water mill. Following a period of political stability the castle was leased in 1488 by a local landowner, Maredudd ap Ieuan, who adapted the keep for residential use.

'Yr uchelwyr' were the families of 'gentle birth' in the medieval and early modern periods, who became the landowners of succeeding centuries. In the case of Dolwyddelan Castle, the family were the Wynns of Gwydir. As Romanticism attracted aristocracy to picturesque ruins in the nineteenth century, Dolwyddelan was partially restored by the Willoughby de Eresby family of Gwydir Castle, Llanrwst. Baron Gwydyr fell in love with the desolate tower on its rocky outcrop above the valley of Afon Ledr and re-roofed the keep, rebuilding the lost battlements that are visible today. Dolwyddelan was copied by Lloyd Hesketh Bamford-Hesketh at Gwrych Castle, and its design was adapted for a brewhouse within the castle complex. The distinctive arrow-loops within the castellations at Dolwyddelan were converted for ventilation in the design at Gwrych.

Today, the castle is in the care of Cadw and, together with Dolbadarn and Prysor, forms a set of native Welsh princes' castles. They all helped secure Llywelyn's mountain kingdom through a network of kinship ties and physical dominance. The castles of Wales, be they English or Welsh in origin, are constant reminders of the medieval struggles for power between a conqueror and the conquered. The Welsh followed their leaders through kinship links; the English were bound together by war and might. The native castles were therefore representative of the Welsh way of life, governing lands that were administered using the Laws of Hywel Dda at a time when ambitions were great but resources limited.

Dolwyddelan holds an evocative place in Welsh history as the reputed birthplace of Prince Llywelyn ab Iorwerth

Plas Teg

Plas Teg

People: Sir John Trevor (1563–1630).

Place: An influential seventeenth-century country house of Sir John Trevor which was a decisive break with traditional Welsh architecture.

Event: Owing largely to Trevor's links with Spain and the court of Phillip III, Plas Teg was the first house in Britain to be designed and built in the classical style, predating Inigo Jones's Queen House at Greenwich by six years. Trevor was one of the most prominent Welsh politicians at the court of James I.

Plas Teg marks a dramatic change in the country house tradition of Wales towards classical design and architecture, a style that would come to dominate the estate buildings of Wales for the next four centuries. Completed around 1610 by Sir John Trevor, it precedes Inigo Jones's Queen House at Greenwich, which has been claimed as Britain's first classical house, by six years. Trevor was a cultured and fashionable member of the Welsh gentry, obtaining important positions at the courts of Elizabeth I and James I. He was at the centre of politics and travelled to Spain in 1605 as part of a peace envoy to Philip III. Trevor was one of Wales' sons who, through kinship connections to the Tudor monarchy, became a wealthy and powerful man. The monies amassed from royal patronage and procurement were invested in his ancestral properties in north Wales where he made his home.

The original medieval hall-house of Plas Teg was celebrated in bardic poetry for its hospitality and the achievements of its owners. This house was replaced by Trevor's classical mansion and the old house became an outbuilding. Trevor was ambitious, not only in his career, but also in the creation of his country estate. The austere classicism is reminiscent of the Spanish royal palaces of the early seventeenth century which Trevor would have seen. Could Wales' first classical house be based upon the architecture

An 1820s engraving of Plas Teg by an unknown artist. The Jacobean gardens were swept away and replaced by a picturesque landscape.

of the sober Catholic works of Juan de Herrera, whose Herrerian was the national form for the Spanish empire?

Francisco de Mora's (c.1553–1610) palaces for Francisco Gómez de Sandoval, 1st Duke of Lerma (1552/1553-1625), the power behind the throne of Phillip III, can be seen in Trevor's Plas Teg. The plain, tall façade, with square corner towers are all in keeping with Herrerian principles, and Plas Teg's general austerity in design contrasts with the elaborate contemporary interiors of the 'prodigy houses' of England's royal courtiers.

The common root for these houses, both in Britain and elsewhere, were the writings of Serlio (1475-c.1554). English court architects, such as John Thorpe (c.1565–1655) may have advised Trevor and drawn up the plans for him, but inspiration appears to have come from Spain. This makes Plas Teg very special, and very unusual. The layout of the house shows a rare form of planning with the great hall and great chamber directly above each other, running from front to back, while the long gallery on the second floor runs side to side. Only a handful of such buildings were built in Britain. Trevor truly wanted Plas Teg to be at the top of its game.

Even though classicism was the influence on the exterior and layout, the interiors of Plas Teg were a showcase for Welsh carpentry. The great oak staircase was executed by the craftsmen of north Wales in true Jacobean style and appears to have influenced staircase design in the area. Elaborate carved strapwork covers

Cornelia Bayley, who purchased the house in 1986.

the stairs and doorcases, mimicking Spanish gilt leather work, and was painted to heighten the relief of the carvings. John Webb (1611-1672), assistant to Inigo Jones, is recorded to have altered Plas Teg during the 1650s for Sir John Trevor II (1596–1673), and may have designed the mid-seventeenth century fireplace in the Great Chamber.

The peak of Plas Teg's prominence was over by the time of Charles II's Restoration, and the house was tenanted. Many of the contents were taken down to Glynde Place, near Lewes, Sussex, where they can be seen to this day. The moving of the family elsewhere preserved the fabric of Plas Teg from later alteration. It was for its state of preservation that a demolition order was overturned in the 1950s, and the building listed. A full restoration was undertaken by Cornelia Bayley in 1986, with the assistance of Cadw.

Mrs. Bayley has spent the last thirty years carefully restoring Trevor's house back to its former glory, establishing an eclectic collection of furniture and forming one of Wales' best private houses. For this reason, Mrs. Bayley's vision for Plas Teg has received international acclaim, putting a rather quiet area outside of Mold on the map. The house has been featured in design books all over the world and has championed the cause of historic building restoration for Wales. It has recently been announced that the house and contents have been gifted to the people of Wales.

Left page: Top: The artist Jonathan Myles-Lea was prompted by Cornelia Bayley to paint his first country house portrait whilst staying at Plas Teg in 1991. This painting launched his career. Bottom left: A copy of a watercolour by Moses Griffith, dated 1783. Due to the financial embarrassment of the the later Trevor family, Plas Teg was preserved in its original classical form. Bottom right: Cornelia Bayley.

A full restoration was undertaken by Cornelia Bayley in 1986, with the assistance of Cadw

Kennixton Farmhouse, originally
built at Llangennith, Gower.

St Fagans National History Museum

St Fagans

People: Earls of Plymouth; Dr Iorwerth Peate (1901-1982).

Place: Originally the Welsh Folk Museum and then the Museum of Welsh Life, the National History Museum at St Fagans is part of National Museum Wales. It chronicles the historical lifestyle, culture and architecture of Wales with an open air collection of buildings and artefacts.

Event: The Earl of Plymouth donated the land in 1946. Peate opened the Welsh Folk Museum in 1948 after visiting the Skansen open-air museum at Stockholm. The museum has come to embody Wales' attachment to its folk heritage.

If fortunate enough to be travelling around Wales you will soon notice that the landscape varies dramatically; from high mountains to rolling hills, forested valleys to wide open plains. It is a joy that a country of just over 8,000 square miles, just smaller than the US state of New Jersey, is home to such great variety of landscape and scenery. Wales can sometimes feel like a small continent of individual countries, each with their own unique character: the dramatic mountains of Snowdonia, the sandy bays of Pembrokeshire, the bleak sculpted hills of the Brecon Beacons.

Just as the landscape changes, so too does the architecture, or at least the traditional architecture built before railways and modern roads encouraged a more uniform approach to design. The vernacular architecture of Wales is a rich collection of buildings that, when 'read' correctly, offers much towards telling the story of the people of Wales. In fact, it can be argued that, even more than this, it is the architecture itself that actually 'built' the Wales of which it so eloquently speaks.

Miners' terraced houses from Rhyd-y-Car, Merthyr Tydfil.

St Fagans formed its core collection of vernacular buildings. As mains electricity and water reached many rural parts in the 1950s, so came great change in the routines of daily life in rural cottages and farms. The staff of St Fagans recognised that people were no longer making their own furniture, they now had machines to help with agricultural and domestic tasks, and the work of the kitchen had changed dramatically. Life got easier, and better in many ways, but an old way of life was disappearing fast. St Fagans set out to record traditional life in all its forms, to preserve what it could and to educate those inside and outside Wales about Welsh culture. More than half a century later and it's easy to see that our country is immensely richer for the great work done by all at the institution.

The museum opened in 1948 in the grounds of the existing Elizabethan manor house at St Fagans, on lands donated by the Earl of Plymouth. The visiting Welsh public would have been familiar with visits to art galleries and museums, castles and great country houses, but to most an open-air museum dedicated to traditional cottages and farmsteads was a novelty. Day-trippers from Cardiff could soon experience a sense of the entirety of rural Wales in a single afternoon's outing.

The museum has given Wales a great pride in itself. Things that were being thrown out or demolished have become celebrated as items of beauty, possessing an intrinsic Welshness, and awarded their rightful place in the national consciousness. People visit St Fagans, see things they recognise from home, from their grandparent's homes, from the

Vernacular buildings are those built without the input of an architect. They tend to follow regional forms, respond to local needs, and use locally available materials to achieve this. Cottages built near the beach may be formed using rounded beach stones; those in areas with a strong timber-frame tradition may be oak-framed; and those in areas of rural poverty without access to good stone or wood may be built from clom, the Welsh mud variant of cob. Each area of Wales has its own overlapping traditions in building form and construction. Yet the traveller doesn't have to traverse the length and breadth of the nation to witness these variants, for just outside Cardiff we have the remarkable museum at St Fagans.

The 1930s idea to create Amgueddfa Werin Cymru, The Welsh Folk Museum, came from Dr Iorwerth Peate. He had been appointed in 1927 to the staff of the Department of Archaeology in the National Museum of Wales with the task of cataloguing what became known as the 'folk collections'. Peate felt a sense of change and loss in rural Wales, and in his work photographing and recording traditional ways of life there is a strong feeling of conservation. He'd spent much of the mid-1930s travelling around Wales recording rural architecture for his 1940 book *The Welsh House*. He was heavily influenced by Scandinavian folk-life recorders and the Skansen open-air museum at Stockholm and, although he initially met with objection to his ideas for establishing a Welsh Skansen, work started in 1946 to create what has become one of Europe's finest institutions. The Welsh Folk Museum has undoubtedly helped form and influence ideas of what Wales and Welshness are.

Rural Wales was undergoing significant change in the mid-twentieth century as shed, and value them. Putting a rack of simple wooden cawl spoons on display in a museum may have seemed unusual in the mid-twentieth century, but now we recognise that these are the kind of objects that help form national identity.

The early buildings reconstructed at St Fagans reflect the rural architecture of Wales: farms and cottages, mills and cow-sheds. They include some remarkable rescue stories, and each is an immaculate reconstruction. Photographs were taken, everything was measured, each visible stone numbered and then reconstructed in perfect detail at the museum site. The very fact that anyone would go to such a high level of care, even mixing mortars using local silts and gravels to get just the right colour, has instilled in the Welsh people a real sense of value for these buildings. As a result we now consider rural and traditional Welsh architecture as something that reflects identity.

Since Peate's time the English name has changed from Welsh Folk Museum to the Museum of Welsh Life and, more recently, to the slightly less satisfactory National History Museum as staff have sought to redress the rural/urban imbalance in the collections. Fortunately, the Welsh title has never changed and remains Amgueddfa Werin Cymru – The Welsh Folk Museum. The abbreviation St Fagans works for most people, irrespective of their language. Today the now iconic buildings of Kennixton Farmhouse and Garreg Fawr have been joined by the Oakdale Workmen's Institute from near Caerphilly and a World War II prefab from Gabalfa in Cardiff. In total more than

forty reconstructed buildings form the heart of the museum's collection, along with new exhibition halls added onto the remodelled visitor centre which was originally, and successfully, designed by Dale Owen for Percy Thomas Partnership between 1968 and 1976.

Wales now has an immense pride in its rural and folk traditions which isn't perhaps as evident in the rest of the United Kingdom. Enter any farmhouse in Carmarthenshire or Ceredigion, even the newly built or renovated ones, and you'd be surprised not to see a traditional dresser loaded with old plates and jugs, probably polished and loved like a family altar. Head up to the north-west and you'll find that many 'tridarn' cupboards remain in the same families they were made for centuries ago, and that others have worked hard, and paid high prices, to buy those that have come up for auction. Such items might stand next to a painting by Sir Kyffin Williams, who represented that same folk tradition in his work and who remains much loved and respected as a result. This story is replicated around Wales, from the continued tradition of giving lovespoons at weddings to the carving of traditional forms on eisteddfodau chairs. In some ways St Fagans reminded people, and continues to do so, how to be Welsh.

Wales may have been the first industrialised nation but it is one that has never forgotten its rural roots. We have St Fagans to thank for that; a centre which has made it acceptable to be proud of the simple architecture and furnishings that make Wales unique. To go there isn't

so much to step back in time to what we were, instead it is a warming reminder of what we are.

The early buildings at St Fagans include some remarkable rescue stories, and each is an immaculate reconstruction

Portmeirion

Portmeirion is a
delicious feast,
like entering a cake
shop full of your
favoured patisserie

Portmeirion

People: Sir Bertram Clough Williams-Ellis (1883-1978).

Place: The Italianate village of Portmeirion on the edge of the Llŷn Peninsula which was developed by Clough Williams-Ellis over the course of 50 years. Now a popular tourist attraction.

Event: Clough Williams-Ellis set out to prove that good architecture could enhance rather than spoil a landscape. In doing so he managed to create one of the most loved locations in the whole of Wales.

Like any other country, the image of Wales has always been defined to an extent by those from outside it – its visitors. People have travelled to Wales for trade and leisure for centuries, and today the tourism industry has grown to become one of the primary sources of income for the nation. For many people, Wales is a place to escape to, and millions flock every year to north-west Wales and the Snowdonia National Park. Here they find the highest mountains in England and Wales, but also a sense of nature and perceived wilderness that is rare in everyday life. Ask anyone from outside Wales to describe the country in a few adjectives and the word 'beautiful' won't

Clough Williams-Ellis.

be far down the list.

The concept of Wales as a holiday destination has been significant in its development and identity, and many buildings could be chosen to represent 'holiday Wales' in a shortlist of those that built the sense of the country. The caravan parks of Cardigan Bay, holiday parks such as Butlins in Pwllheli, the beautiful sweep of hotels on Llandudno promenade, and the amusements on Barry Island all played their part in creating the image of Wales as a place to enjoy and relax. At Portmeirion near Penrhyndeudraeth you'll find something very special.

This beautiful bay, filled with a fantasy mix of traditional architecture in cheerful Mediterranean colours, feels like a trip into a British filmset representation of an Italian village from the mid-twentieth century. It's no surprise that it has often been used as a set, most notably for the now cult 1960s TV series *The Prisoner*, where what appeared to be a giant inflated ball chased actor Patrick McGoohan around the streets of this holiday village. Only in Portmeirion could such a bizarre fantasy appear feasible.

Portmeirion was the pet project of Sir Bertram Clough Williams-Ellis who developed the site from 1925 to 1976. It is a village of fantasy holiday cottages and other structures centred around a hotel on the beautiful estuary of the Dwyryd River. Clough was an English-born architect/designer and writer of Welsh descent, who despite having no formal training in the field, became a successful 'country house' architect in the inter-war years.

Clough was a wonderful and prolific polymath, interested in the environment, design and conservation. He was a founding member of the Council for the Protection of Rural England (1926), the Campaign for the Protection of Rural Wales (1928), a campaigner for National Parks in England and Wales, and was the man who presented his demarcation of the Snowdonia National Park boundary to King George VI and Queen Elizabeth in 1951. The interest in good design runs in the family, and Clough's eldest daughter Susan (1918-2007), was one of Britain's finest twentieth-century commercial

ceramic designers. Clough's brand of architecture is unique, but can be loosely understood within the Arts & Crafts genre. While the big names in inter-war architecture were turning to modernism, Clough's first love was the architecture and detailing of historic periods. That said, the way in which he brought together the Baroque and Rococo, the vernacular and the formal, all in one village makes him a pioneer of post-modern architectural values. Ultimately, he escapes pigeon-holing; Portmeirion is a one-off, and it is wonderful.

Portmeirion appears to have grown organically in a whimsical manner with little formal planning. Clough added a statue here, a colonnade there, and the village benefitted significantly from architectural salvage available after the bombing raids of World War II. Clough had the good fortune of working in an environment in which he could create whatever he wished on his own private peninsula. Many would have opted for commercial gain and built nondescript mass holiday housing to create maximum profit, but Clough was an aesthete and creating Portmeirion was his labour of love. The village that he created is a commercial success both for day visitors and the guests who choose to make it their holiday home. Although its growth appears to have been according to supply of materials and funds, there is also a planned theme throughout the whole. Clough bought thirty 'mermaids' from Liverpool and used these as a repeated motif throughout the village, and used the 'Portmeirion Green', a turquoise/green paint, as the estate colour.

The term 'Italianate' is often used to describe Portmeirion, and it is true that the overall impression of the place is more Mediterranean than Meirionydd, with its tropical planting and colour-washed walls. Yet a closer look reveals that a single building can reference East Anglia as easily as Portofino in Italy. Clough wasn't trying to recreate Italy any more than he was trying to reconstruct specific buildings: he was playing with architecture, mixing motifs and designs to create something wonderful, and new. Much of it may have been happy accident, determined by available materials. In fact it is remarkable that Portmeirion works as a piece of architecture, but it does, and it has certainly become something more than the sum of its irregular parts.

Ultimately, Portmeirion is Welsh. It is something unique to its own location, and it is a place of fantasy so delightful that there will never be a shortage of day visitors who come to marvel at the architecture and designed vistas. Many have made a pilgrimage to Portmeirion for inspiration: Noel Coward wrote *Blithe Spirit* in one of the cottages, and American architect Frank Lloyd Wright made a special visit in 1956.

Portmeirion is a delicious feast, like entering a cake shop full of your favoured patisserie made in new combinations. The palm trees are preposterous, and yet they seem at home here. Each corner holds a new delight. Portmeirion is hyper-real, too-perfect and yet wonderful in the way it 'gilds the lily' of architecture.

Clough said that he built Portmeirion to show how architecture can enhance the landscape rather than spoil it. There is no doubt that he succeeded. Often people object to any building in an open landscape, without first considering what the building brings to the place and its sense of place. We need more Cloughs in the architectural scene of today; a little more of his sense of whimsy would do no great harm.

Llwynywermod

Llwynywermod

People: Griffies-Williams family; the Prince of Wales.

Place: Llwynywermod is the Welsh residence of the Prince of Wales.

Event: Purchased by the Duchy of Cornwall in 2006.

The origins of the secluded estate of Llwynywermod, historically known as Llwynywormwood, are obscure, though its name is a clue. Wormwood was a medicinal herb used widely in the medieval and early modern periods for keeping away moths and fleas. One may hypothesise that the famed Physicians of Myddfai, so-called fathers of modern medicine, were linked in some way to the 'Grove of Wormwood', but whatever the truth may be, this little piece of Carmarthenshire is enigmatic, rich in ancient tales and stories. The Lady of the Lake from Arthurian legend is said to dwell in the nearby lake of Llyn-y-Fan Fach.

The Williams family were early owners of Llwynywermod built a sixteenth-century manor house on an eminence overlooking a sheltered valley, with views out to the Black Mountain and Carmarthenshire Fan. This Tudor mansion was built into the hillside for protection.

By the late eighteenth century, the estate had passed sideways to a collateral

Sir Erasmus Griffies-Williams, the last hereditary owner of Llwynywermod to live at the house. When he died suddenly his final work was an unpublished dictionary of Welsh to English.

branch of the family, the Griffies from Brecon, and in order to inherit as well as preserve the name Williams, they hyphenated their surnames. The Griffies-Williamses set about transforming the park into a picturesque landscape by damming the streams flowing through the valley to create lakes, building bridges for a new carriage drive that wound through the park, on the brow of the opposing hillside, to the main house. They planted hundreds of deciduous and non-deciduous trees to form an extensive designed landscape. Still, even though the grounds could have been picked from a northern Italian palazzo, the rambling, ancient manor house remained its central feature.

Through its architecture, Llwynywermod

told the story of the Welsh gentry, a story one can find repeated throughout Wales. They were never ostensibly rich or extravagant but continued to farm the land of their ancestors for centuries, adding to their homes pragmatically. The more stylish folk would add a fashionable canted bay, or even re-front an earlier house, all of which can be seen in the surviving historic imagery of Llwynywermod. The pedigree roll of the Griffies-Williamses was said to be so long that, when it was laid out, it stretched the full length of the house.

Agriculture was the bread and butter income for the estates of Wales. At Llwynywermod a quadrangle of outbuildings were constructed, intended to look like a picturesque estate village,

The gentle Lady Caroline Griffies-Williams, wife of Erasmus, photographed here shortly before her death.

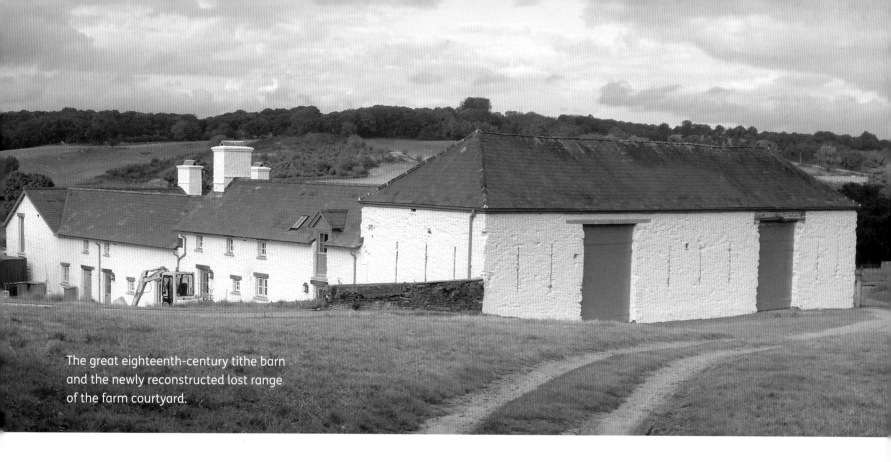

The great eighteenth-century tithe barn and the newly reconstructed lost range of the farm courtyard.

with the second largest tithe barn in Carmarthenshire. Such visual prominence to farm buildings was no accident; the Griffies-Williamses were proud of their farming and were at the forefront of agriculture reform in the early nineteenth century.

From the 1870s onwards the estate was slowly dismantled, with sales every few years reducing it in size and extent, so by the last sale in 1909 the house was empty and the last portion of the park put up for auction. For most of the twentieth century the house was used for quarry, being easy pickings for rebuilding field boundaries and hardcore for modern farm buildings. In the 1990s, the Hegartys purchased what was essentially a working farm with dilapidated garden features, but one with the underlying structure of a forgotten

picturesque landscape still intact.

The Duchy of Cornwall, on behalf of the Prince of Wales, had been seriously searching for the perfect house and estate for the Prince and his family. By chance they stumbled on the work undertaken by the Hegartys in unpicking a century of neglect at Llwynywermod. The Prince and the Duchess of Cornwall visited one summer's day in 2006 and fell in love with its evocative location. Within a year the estate had been purchased. Craig Hamilton drew up the designs to restore the farm quadrangle, rebuilding the north range in its entirety as it had been previously demolished in favour of a steel cattle shed. With due care and attention, using traditional building materials and techniques, the courtyard one again featured a kitchen garden at its centre.

The Prince uses Llwynywermod as a base for his Welsh visits, as well as a centre for his charitable interests. What lies in store for the ruins of the old mansion one can only imagine. But one retains a hope that someday the illustrious home of the ancient Griffies-Williams family might be rebuilt. Similar to Hafod, near Devil's Bridge, the whole parkland and designed landscape was originally formed around the house at its centre. Can the old heart of Llwynywermod be revived once more?

Little remains of the old mansion of Llwynywermod except for the forlorn, asset-stripped ruins of two side elevations.

Broadcasting House, Llandaff

Wales has seen the loss of many of its great twentieth-century buildings as the government and nation have sometimes been slow to recognise their value. Gone is the remarkable Brynmawr rubber factory, one of the finest examples of post-war architecture in Europe, to make way for an unsuccessful housing scheme. Gone is the wonderful Empire Pool in Cardiff as it occupied the intended building site of the Principality Stadium (a cinema now stands there instead). Bettws High School may have been considered the finest new architecture in Wales in 1972 but it has now been replaced following its demolition in 2010. The Knap Lido at Barry has been filled in. Countless good inter-war cinemas of Deco Moderne design have been demolished, and not a single prefab built in the aftermath of World War II was afforded protection, despite many surviving half a century after they were built and being much loved by residents. Penarth has lost its modernist Esplanade Car Park and, in 2013, the much loved 1979 Chartist mural in Newport was controversially demolished.

Next to go is one that we can consider to have built modern Wales: BBC Broadcasting House in Llandaff. This has been the centre of national broadcasting in Wales since it was constructed to a sensitive design by Dale Owen of Percy Thomas partnership. It was opened in 1966, and consists of three blocks of purpose-built studios, offices and technical facilities covering a large, well-landscaped site with excellent transport links and parking. It is among the finest commercial architecture from mid-century Wales, and is by one of Wales' greatest architects.

It is among the finest commercial architecture from mid-century Wales, and is by one of Wales' greatest architects

Broadcasting House

People: Architect, Dale Owen (1924-1997) of Percy Thomas.

Place: Broadcasting House, Llandaff. Home to BBC Wales between 1966 and 2018, when the organisation is scheduled to move to new offices designed by Norman Foster in central Cardiff.

Event: The centre of national broadcasting in Wales since it opened in 1966.

What is successful about Broadcasting House is that a different form is given to each of the various functions of the building

Dale Owen worked with Walter Gropius, founder of the Bauhaus, and was architect of the National Museum of Wales at St Fagan's (1968-81) and the Arts Centre at Aberystwyth (1970-72), as well as the University of Wales campus developments in Swansea, Aberystwyth and Cardiff. He lived in one of Wales' finest 1930s Moderne villas on the seafront at Penarth, and was a kind and generous individual. Owen was interested in both heritage protection and supporting young architects; he fully backed Zaha Hadid's ill-fated Cardiff opera-house proposal.

What is successful about Broadcasting House is that a different form is given to each of the various functions of the building. The long, low-rise canteen floats on stilts adjacent to the taller offices. Small studios extend along the roadside and Studio One rises high against the street elevation. Broadcasting House is considered fit for purpose and a strong piece of modernist architecture in concrete stone and glass. Owen never swayed from Bauhaus principles and recalled with delight his victory in persuading the BBC to buy real Mies van der Rohe chairs for the reception area.

The first radio broadcast from Wales was in 1923. Television was broadcast from 1952, and, in 1957, BBC West started to produce a short news bulletin on Wales from Bristol. It wasn't until 1964 that BBC Wales was established, providing a broadcaster for the nation of Wales against a background of increased devolution in the decade when Wales was finally taken seriously by London. The Percy Thomas building was commissioned to house the new institution, and for decades BBC Cymru Wales has produced television and radio in English and Welsh from there.

The first colour television broadcast came from Broadcasting House in Llandaff in 1970. The building was home to the National Orchestra of Wales and the National Chorus of Wales. *Doctor Who, Torchwood, Casualty* and *Crimewatch*. Welsh and English language news services have all been produced in Broadcasting House. For decades it was home to the permanent *Pobl y Cwm* sets; the long-running Welsh language soap that can have a claim in the survival and success of the language as the most watched programme on S4C.

In 2013 BBC Wales announced that the building no longer suited its purpose as it had 'out-dated technology'. Rather than upgrade, the decision has been made to sell the valuable site in Llandaff in order to move to a prime spot on the proposed Central Square. While most headquarters move away from the centre as institutions mature, BBC Wales appears to be bucking the trend and moving onto what could be the most expensive piece of land in the history of Wales. As the Welsh language provider S4C is devolving its headquarters to Carmarthen in order to connect with the people of Wales, BBC Wales is moving into the city centre.

At the news of the potential loss of Broadcasting House, the Twentieth Century Society put out a statement saying: 'The BBC building is one of Wales' most outstanding and important Modernist buildings, and one of the best remaining examples of this highly significant Welsh architectural practice.'

Others pointed to how the 1950s former BBC Television Centre in west London had also recently closed, yet had been sensitively developed for housing, hotel and office space; uses that may well be suitable for Llandaff. The current plan in Cardiff is to sell to Taylor Wimpey who plan to demolish and build four hundred new homes on the current headquarters site.

Cadw recommended the structure for listing on the basis of its special architectural interest

Cadw recommended the structure for listing on the basis of its special architectural interest 'as a sensitively designed complex of buildings by one of Wales' leading modernist architects, and as an exemplary modernist building. It is also of special historic interest as the only purpose-built national public service broadcasting centre of its period in Wales'. The Welsh Government rejected Cadw's recommendation for listing in 2014, stating that, in their opinion, it did not meet the criteria for a building of special architectural or historic interest.

The move to the new BBC headquarters on Central Square is scheduled for 2018 and will mark a shift in Welsh broadcasting, away from one where the BBC commissions and produces its own output to one where that production is increasingly outsourced to private companies. The new headquarters will have only half the floor-space of the old. It can therefore only be hoped that, while its impact on Welsh architectural heritage is perhaps not to the best advantage, the decision taken by the BBC will permit Wales to retain a strong, independent and unique voice within broadcasting in the UK.

Gregynog

Gregynog

People: Gwendoline Davies (1882-1951) and her sister Margaret, known as Daisy (1884-1963).

Place: The Davies sisters purchased Gregynog Hall in 1920, one of Montgomeryshire's leading landed estates at Tregynon, near Newtown.

Event: The intention was to create an arts and crafts centre for Wales, to enrich popular understanding of art, music and poetry. The long-term effect has indeed been an enrichment of the culture of Wales.

In 1920 Gwendoline Davies and her sister Margaret, known as Daisy, purchased one of Montgomeryshire's leading landed estates at Tregynon, near Newtown in Montgomeryshire. Their intention was to create an arts and crafts centre for Wales. The Davies sisters were aware that their great wealth, via their grandfather David Davies of Llandinam, a significant Welsh coal and docks entrepreneur, was owed to the labours of the working classes. The sisters felt they should make an enduring gift to the people of Wales. The vehicle for their various endeavours was Gregynog, a cultural centre to for art, music and creative skills. As such this country house estate became a unique social experiment.

The Davies sisters, with their brother David, a Liberal MP for Montgomeryshire, were remarkable philanthropists who had already donated large sums to good causes before the Gregynog project began. During the First World War they ran a canteen for the French Red

Gwendoline Davies

Margaret Davies

Cross. They decided to enrich popular understanding of art, music and poetry, and the long-term effect has been an undoubted enrichment of the culture of Wales.

A house has existed at Gregynog since the Middle Ages, but the majority of what you see on the outside today is concrete over brick added in 1872. Inside is a house mostly rebuilt in 1840 which reuses the panelling of its seventeenth-century predecessor in the dining room. The estate was one of the pioneers of the use of concrete in Welsh building, using it for bridges, cottages and farm buildings. The concrete façade of the main house is heavily decorated in black and white to reflect the local timber-frame architectural tradition, yet is entirely solid

masonry and cement, and not timber as it appears from a distance. The Davies sisters converted the billiard room into a music room for their famous festivals of music and poetry. They attracted composers such as Holst, Vaughan Williams and Elgar.

Gwendoline and Daisy had a passion for art, and in particular French Impressionists and post-Impressionists, and even before the war they'd started to amass an important collection of paintings and other works, including Monet, Cézanne, Pissarro, Renoir and Van Gogh. They gradually built one of most significant private art collections in Europe. That they managed to purchase so many works that are now considered world-class art is partly due to their

advisers but more to their genuine understanding and appreciation for French and British art.

The sisters bequeathed some 260 artworks to the National Museum of Wales in 1951 and 1963, making Cardiff a destination on the international art scene. These include three of Monet's *Waterlilies* paintings, Renoir's *La Parisienne* and Rodin's sculpture *The Kiss*. The sisters had also collected the best British twentieth-century artists such as Eric Gill, Augustus John, Stanley Spencer and Frank Brangwyn. Almost every gallery in Cardiff contains some of their donations today. Gregynog Hall itself was gifted to the University of Wales in 1960.

Among the many creative endeavours of the Davies sisters was the establishment

of the Gregynog Press. Founded in 1922, the press set out to publish high-quality art tomes using original commissioned wood-cuts and engravings. In its inter-war heyday it produced some of the finest luxury illustrated books in Britain, employing leading engravers and illustrators of the time such as Agnes Miller Parker. Most were printed in limited editions and have become collector pieces.

The sisters donated the contents of the press to the National Library of Wales in 1954, and the University of Wales re-launched the printing house as Gwasg Gregynog in 1978. It continues to publish beautifully created and illustrated books in both languages, and had a particularly successful collaboration with the late Sir Kyffin Wiliams. The press was commissioned to produce the inaugural document for the opening of the National Assembly for Wales and another special edition for the opening of the Senedd.

That the house at Gregynog was a pioneer in the use of concrete was lucky coincidence, as the site deserved inclusion in this volume by virtue of being a centre for Welsh culture alone.

Almost a century after the sisters moved to the estate we can see that Wales as a whole has benefitted from their contribution, with the National Museum, the Welsh College of Music, the National Library and the University of Wales all the richer because of them. They brought world-class art and music to Wales, and disseminated the culture of Wales back to the world through Gregynog Press.

Founded in 1922, the Gregynog press set out to publish high-quality art tomes using original commissioned woodcuts and engravings

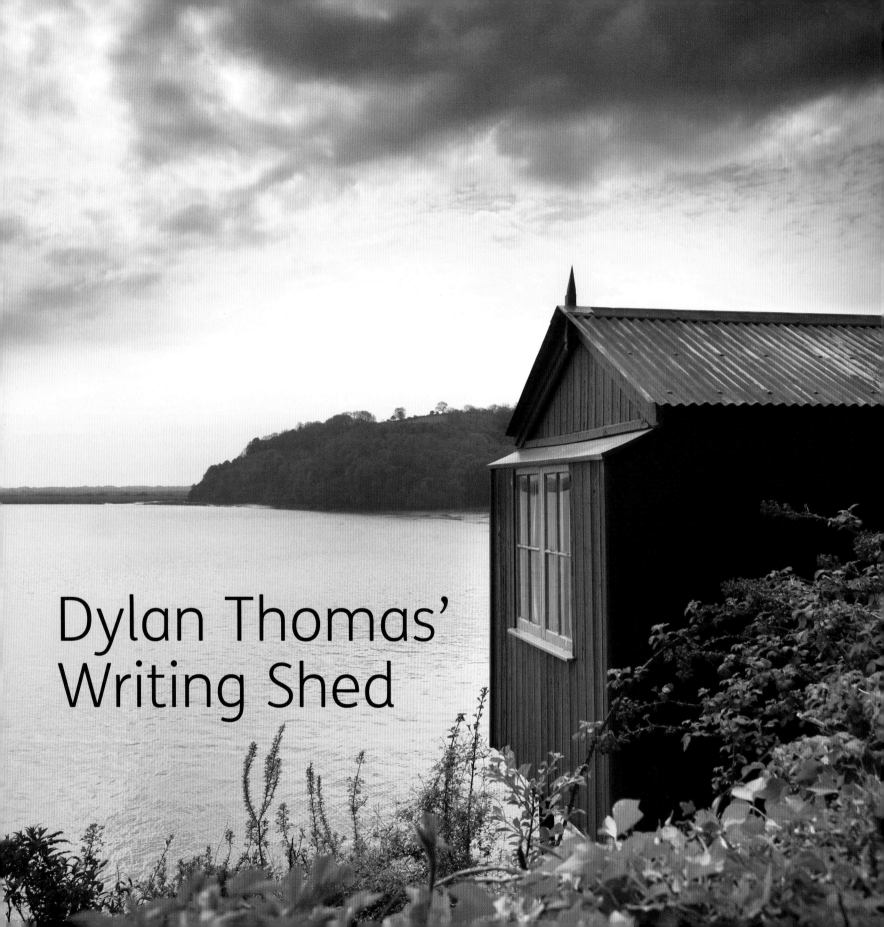

Dylan Thomas'
Writing Shed

The humblest building in our selection is a simple wooden shed, one not dissimilar to the kind of shed you might purchase from any garden centre today. It is a structure that has become associated with the celebrated writer Dylan Thomas, a largely rebuilt version of the garage he wrote from during the last four years of his life. Dylan is loved around the world for his poems including *Do not go gentle into that good night*, plays such as *Under Milk Wood* and radio broadcasts such as *A Child's Christmas in Wales*. As such he has penned an image of Wales that has been influential in the way others see our country. Today the simple shed he used for writing has become iconic, both of Thomas himself and of the wider concept of Anglo-Welsh literature.

Dylan's relationship with Wales and Welshness is a complex one, and it could be argued that he is isn't a worthy hero for the nation. His terrible drunkenness and infidelity shocked the principled values of west Wales' chapel culture, and he left a string of debts everywhere he lived. But if it is difficult to love Dylan as a person, it isn't difficult to love his work, which is among the finest twentieth-century writing to come out of Britain.

Dylan (pronounced 'Dillon to rhyme with 'villain', he insisted, not the more correct 'Duhlan') created a caricature vision of rural Wales in his writing. The play *Under Milk Wood* in particular become so popular after his death that many outsiders imagine that rural Wales is entirely like his fictional 'Llareggub' (read it backwards to get an idea of his feelings about rural Wales). Tourists come, following the Thomas trail in New Quay, Laugharne

and the 'ugly, lovely' city of Swansea (his words) where he retains iconic status.

The possession of a writing shed is a great asset in the public image of any serious writer. Henry Thoreau had one, Virginia Woolf had one, and Welsh writer Roald Dahl had one. Our romanticised image of the writer dictates that we expect them to have a shed in the garden in which to find the peace to create their great works. We want them to be alone, writing with pen or pencil, to be slightly tortured, throwing scraps of drafts away, and we want them to be inspired by a great open view. And we want to be able to visit the place for ourselves so that we can try to access the same ambience that inspired the great works created there. It isn't hard, then, to see why the blue painted 1930s garage used by Dylan as he pursed his 'craft or sullen art' has proved so popular.

The hut Thomas used as a writing shed has been rebuilt and refurnished according to old photographs, with the façade of the original now standing in the Dylan Thomas Centre in Swansea. The garage had been built in timber by Dr Cowan of Oxford in the 1930s who used the Boathouse as his holiday home. He wanted somewhere under cover to house his Wolseley, one of the first cars in Laugharne. Visitors today will see a representation of the 1950s as screwed up papers litter the floor, pictures on the wall curl in the dampness, and 'Dylan's' coat hangs off the back of the chair; all as if he's just popped over to Brown's Hotel for a pint, or ten. A bottle of beer sits on the main desk.

Dylan Thomas' Writing Shed

People: Dylan Thomas (1914-1953) and Caitlin Thomas (1913–1994).

Place: What is now known as the Writing Shed in Laugharne is where author Dylan Thomas worked during the last four years of his life. Now managed by Carmarthenshire County Council, it is a major tourist attraction in south-west Wales.

Event: With its unparalleled views across four estuaries, the Writing Shed is not just a present location; rather it has become an icon associated with Wales' most famous literary figure.

An iconic symbol
of Welsh writing

The picture may be inaccurate however. In *Portrait of Dylan*, a photographic memoir by Rollie McKenna, the only images of Thomas in his shed show a tidy space with two desks, so the poet could sit in front of either window. The main window faces out to the River Taf and the south-facing window over to Llansteffan. The opening stanza of *Poem on his Birthday* describes his estuary view:

In the mustardseed sun,
By full tilt river and switchback sea
Where the cormorants scud,
In his house on stilts high among beaks
And palavers of birds

In the late 1970s the management of the building passed to the Rural District Council (now Carmarthenshire County Council) and the writing shed and house are now open as a popular tourist attraction and place of pilgrimage. It is hard to peer inside the hut and not be slightly jealous of the fine view, the simple interior and the peace and quiet it holds within.

Whatever our thoughts about Dylan, we cannot deny he was a gifted writer. And whether or not we want Wales to be caricatured as he did, we cannot change the fact that Wales has become defined

by his work, nor that the blue wooden shed he worked in has become a symbol of Welsh writing more generally. In 2014 a replica of the shed went on tour, travelling throughout Wales and even over to Ireland as part of the 'Dylan 100' celebrations which marked the centenary of his birth in 1914. As part of the romanticisation of Thomas we celebrate his simple writing shed, and as time goes on we perhaps remember less the man himself and more the writing he gave us.

National Library
of Wales

Many scholars head to Aberystwyth due to the rich resource that is the National Library. Treasures, once confined to private Welsh country house libraries, can now be found within the offices and on the shelves of the National Library, and are available for public consumption. The building itself, constructed around the corner from Aberystwyth University and overlooking the seafront sweep of the town, is palatial and arguably has one of the best views of any institution in Wales. The collections are so diverse, from the papers of many great estates to personal photographs of members of the Gorsedd. It is probably one of the lesser known gems of Wales' tourist destinations.

The story of the National Library began with a bitter fight. Cardiff wanted the institution, Aberystwyth was the opponent. What appears to have swung

Sir John Williams.

matters in Aberystwyth's favour was Sir John Williams, whose great collection included the Peniarth manuscripts. He offered to donate his papers, which were recognised to be of international importance, to the proposed National Library only if it was based in Aberystwyth. He refused to let it go to Cardiff. It was not all bad news as Cardiff gained the National Museum. Both the library and the museum were established by Royal Charter in 1907.

Sidney Greenslade was appointed architect and the design for the Library was chosen in 1909. Monies were raised in various ways, and the miners of south Wales contributed one shilling each. Greenslade was assisted by Reginald Bloomfield and the building they constructed was first occupied in 1916, during the height of the First World War. It was a confident building, offering defiance against the tragedies occurring in continental Europe. Over the next forty years the building evolved, with various additions expanding the space available for ever-growing collections. Its exterior is faced with Portland stone and Cornish granite, and would easily appear at home among the contemporary civic buildings of Cathays Park, Cardiff. Its design is a mix of fashionable Art Deco and Classical Greek Revival – an eye on the current, yet also casting a glance to the past. A collection of Brynmawr Quaker furniture has pride of place in the Library's board room. The Brynmawr Furniture Makers were established in 1929 by Peter Scott and lasted eleven years, their aim being to alleviate unemployment in the industrialised area of Brynmawr.

North Reading Room

National Library of Wales

People: Sir John Williams (1840-1926), philanthropist; Sidney Greenslade (1867-1955), architect.

Place: Established by Royal Charter in 1907 and first occupied in 1916, the National Library of Wales in Aberystwyth today houses 6.5 million volumes and is the legal depositary for all printed works. It is also home to the National Screen and Sound Archive.

Event: Wales' status as a literary nation was strengthened when the National Library was founded at the start of the twentieth century; bringing together manuscript collections of international importance and making them available to the public.

Today, the library is the legal deposit for all printed works. Their collection now numbers over 6.5 million volumes and is continuing to expand. Its most famous manuscripts include the first book printed in Welsh, *Yny Ihyvyr hwnn* (1546) and the medieval *Black Book of Carmarthen*. The National Screen and Sound Archive of Wales is also located there, gathering as much as it can from the more modern history of Wales and committed to saving rare recordings for posterity. Digitisation has been a major investment for the library, with over fifty titles from Welsh journals now available online for users to peruse from anywhere in the world.

Wales is a literary nation, and the National Library of Wales continues to play an important role in the cultural and educational life of its people. It protects a physical collection of diverse artefacts relating to Wales and the other Celtic nations. Its continuing aims are to collect and preserve the intellectual record of Wales and to give access to a wide variety of people. Long may it continue to do so.

Left: The Vaux Passional, from the Peniarth manuscripts, currently held in the library's collections. Seen is Henry VII receiving this manuscript as a gift. In the background to the top left is Henry VIII as a child weeping over the death of his mother. His sisters, Mary and Margaret, sit in the foreground. Circa 1503-1504.

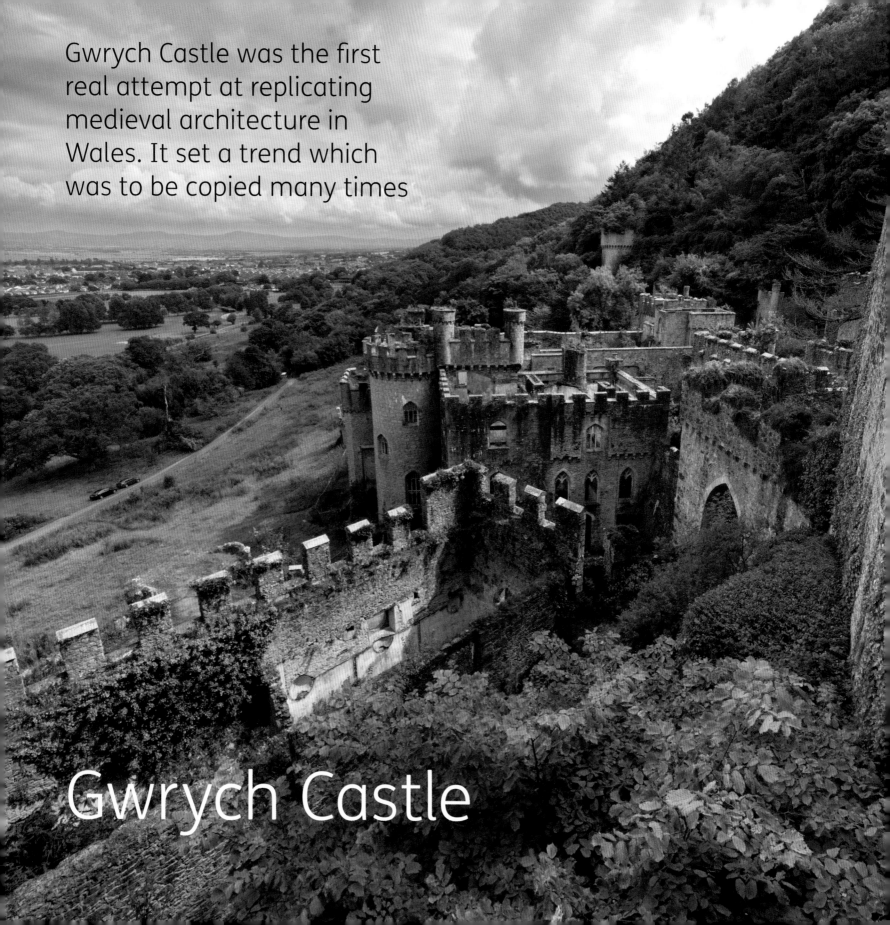

Gwrych Castle was the first real attempt at replicating medieval architecture in Wales. It set a trend which was to be copied many times

Gwrych Castle

Lloyd Hesketh Bamford-Hesketh was his own architect, and built Gwrych as an homage to his mother's family, the ancient Lloyds of Gwrych.

Gwrych Castle was lauded as one of the nineteenth century's largest newly built structures in Europe, and also one of the most engraved buildings in Wales. It was copied many times, particularly in north Wales, where Gothic truly won in the 'Battle of Styles' against neoclassicism. As an example of the architecture of ancestry, Gwrych was homage to a Welsh gentry narrative which had been the grain and patina of Wales since the late-medieval period.

In the 1790s a young boy had a dream of building a monument in memory of his mother's ancestors, the Lloyds of Gwrych. This young boy was the evocatively named Lloyd Hesketh Bamford-Hesketh, heir to the ancient estate of Gwrych. A grand tour travelling through France, Germany, Italy and Egypt fuelled him with a desire to build, but the question arose, in what style? He mused and considered the options, and decided that his inspiration lay in the land of his mother, Wales.

On Hesketh's return he set about surveying the medieval castles of north Wales, such as Rhuddlan, Beaumaris, Conwy, Dolbadarn and Dolwyddelan, carefully measuring their dimensions, dissecting their construction techniques and on his estate he began to experiment. At first he was not confident in his own designs and, in 1813, commissioned Charles Augustus Busby (1786-1834) to produce a plan and sketch of a castellated mansion. Busby's effort lacked imagination but it spurred Hesketh enough to realise his own plans. Hesketh was, out of necessity, a pragmatist as his income was rather meagre, being mostly from land rents and inheritance from distant relations. For the build he utilised

Gwrych Castle

People: Lloyd Hesketh Bamford-Hesketh (1789-1861) and his granddaughter Winifred, Countess of Dundonald (1859-1924).

Place: Gwrych Castle, Abergele, one of Europe's largest structures built in the nineteenth century. It was one of the first romantic ruins to be deliberately constructed and it became pivotal in shaping Wales' relationship with its past.

Event: An example of the architecture of ancestry, Gwrych Castle was an attempt by Lloyd Hesketh Bamford-Hesketh to pay homage to his maternal forbears and replicate the medieval castles of Wales.

the high quality limestone around Gwrych, quarrying and building literally metres apart, in a truly medieval fashion. He reopened Roman lead mines on the estate with a view to keeping everything as local as possible. Hesketh was one of the first to attempt to recreate medieval building techniques in an accurate way.

Gothic stone windows proved too costly to fit out the castle so he approached Liverpool-based architect and architectural antiquary, Thomas Rickman (1776-1841), who advised that Hesketh could achieve the same effect as wood or stone with cast iron, but without the cost or time involved. The stained glass recorded the evocative descent of the Welsh gentry from the Noble Tribes of

During World War II, Jewish refugee children were brought to Gwrych as part of Operation Kindertransport.

north Wales. Hesketh also struggled with building a circular tower so, in 1817, Rickman provided a suggested methodology which Hesketh used to great effect, building at least eighteen towers at the main building at Gwrych.

For fifty years, Hesketh continued to expand the castle so, by the time of his death, Hesketh's granddaughter, the Welsh-speaking Countess of Dundonald, continued in the family tradition of building. She added an elaborate marble staircase in 1914, to the designs of Detmar Blow (1867-1939). The Gwrych Castle Preservation Trust was founded in 2001 and has been tirelessly working towards the rescue of the castle. Today, the castle is a ruin but is slowly being resurrected by the Trust and the the current owners of Gwrych, EPM UK.

Above: Winifred, Countess of Dundonald, was the last of the Lloyds of Gwrych and a fervent Welshwoman, leaving the castle to the nation on her death in 1924.

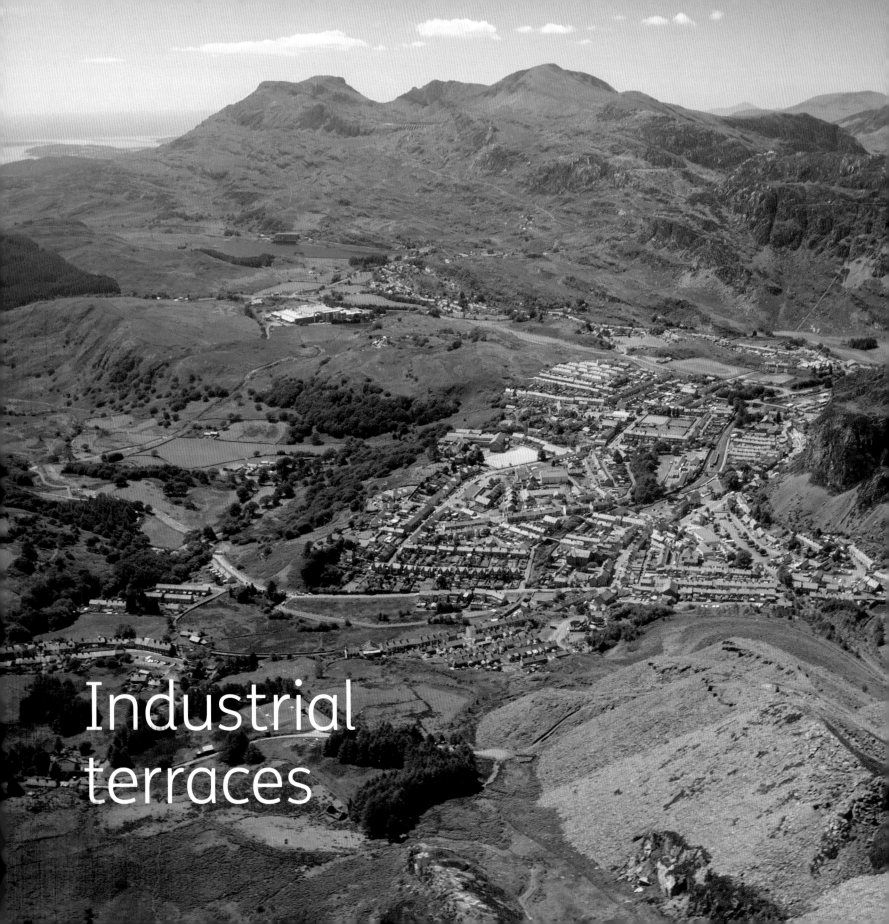

Industrial
terraces

Although Wales feels like an essentially rural nation today, it can claim to be the world's first industrial nation in that it was the first country in the world where more people were employed in industrial work than agriculture. This occurred as early as 1850. Wales is a small country rich in mineral resources and was an early starter in the Industrial Revolution, exporting copper, steel and iron, coal, slate and granite. As these industries boomed in various parts of Wales a need grew for affordable, compact housing for workers, and so developed the standardised terraced house form of industrial workers' housing. These terraces and the people who live in them have added in no small measure to international perceptions of our country.

You'll find terraced industrial workers' housing in many parts of Britain, but in Wales the repetition of standardised terraced house designs has led to industrial terraces becoming synonymous with Welsh architecture and landscape. When outsiders think how Wales looks they tend to picture either mountain wilderness, usually populated by sheep, or row upon row of tightly packed industrial terraces lining steep green hillsides. You don't have to travel far in Wales to find examples of these terraces that are so common as to seem unremarkable today.

When you consider that the population of Wales almost quadrupled during the nineteenth century, from around 600,000 in 1801 to over two million in 1901, and that the population increase was largely due to the development of the South Wales Valleys (Glamorgan witnessed a ten-fold increase in population from

Industrial Terraces

People: The industrial terraces of Blaenau Ffestiniog were the homes of the workers of the great slate industry and continue to provide well-built houses for the people of the town.

Place: Nestled within the shadows of Snowdonia and the steep ramparts of discarded slate, the stronghold of Blaenau Ffestiniog still inspires awe in those who visit and experience the drama of our industrial past.

Event: Welsh slate was a prized commodity which was shipped all over the world to roof the buildings of the ever-expanding British Empire. The slate quarries were an economic force to be reckoned with and saw a great influx of settlers to the area during the nineteenth century.

71,000 in 1801 to 860,000 in 1901) it is easy to see why there was demand for efficient mass-housing. The great Welsh historian John Davies in his excellent book *The Making of Wales* commented that:

'of all the achievements of the makers of Wales between 1850 and 1914, the greatest was to house the population'.

Industrial terraces feel so familiar that to describe them seems almost unnecessary. Typically when you visit a terraced house you know where the kitchen and bathroom are placed without having to ask. The front door generally enters a small lobby from which a straight run of stairs lead up to the first floor bedrooms. The front street-side room

will be the most formal, or only living room and, if there is a second, this will be less formal and possibly converted to a dining area. The kitchen will be to the rear, often with the bathroom above upstairs, though many retain ground floor bathrooms in rear 'outshots'. The primary bedroom will be to the front and there will be either one or two others depending on the arrangement. Rarely are there four bedrooms and rarely is the loftspace used in the original configuration. Houses tended to be uniformly single-fronted with one door and one window to the

ground floor, two upstairs, though there are comparatively rare examples of early back to back houses and a few double-fronted examples.

We're so familiar with it today that it is easy to overlook just how ingenious the terraced design is. Few countries in Europe have such tightly packed single-property accommodation and many on the continent consider the terraced house to be a uniquely British design. The use of space is clever, as is the way they save on building materials and heating; a mid-terrace house will naturally be

warmer than an end-of terrace. Despite the fact that they were often built fast and cheaply for rent by private landlords, the industrial terraces of Wales tend to be well built and with better soundproofing than properties being built today.

The terraced-house plan replaced the tradition of dense slum housing where infill courts were inserted to the rear of existing housing. These tended to be poorly designed, had low light levels and non-existent water and sewage arrangements. The terraced design is partly the result of local bye-laws that stipulated minimum road widths and the space between houses, and that drainage be provided. One simple long row was a cost-effective solution and a great improvement on courtyard dwellings. Most terraces were built not by industrialists directly but by small-scale speculators who often built on leased land. These were often local business people or even the local vicar. Friendly Societies and investing bodies made loans available to speculators to construct terraces that would be rented to the people moving in to work in the mine or quarry. In some cases, such as Llanberis, terraced houses were commissioned by the quarry-workers or bought by them directly from the builders. As much of the land in industrial areas was owned by large landholders the terraces were often built leasehold, and sometimes with oppressive contracts that meant anything built on the land reverted to the landlord at the end of the lease.

The people who moved into industrial terraced housing varied from area to area. In the north Wales quarries the workers tended to be from north Wales and so retained their Welsh speaking community. Some even maintained their rural cottages as well and rented a terraced house near to their place of work. You also find brick terraced weavers' housing in mid Wales dating from 1780-1820 with large cast-iron windows to allow long working days at the home loom. The South Wales Valleys saw such speedy expansion in the late nineteenth century that there was massive immigration from England, something which has influenced their character and use of English to this day. Up until 1890 most of the

migration tended to be from rural Wales, but after this point there was significant immigration from England, Ireland and Scotland.

Despite being the most common housing type in Wales it is remarkably difficult to find examples of Welsh industrial workers' housing that haven't seen significant alteration. County Council renovation grant schemes have stripped whole valleys of traditional windows and slate roofs, removing chimneys and adding render and pebbledash. A typical view of a valleys terrace today will show more individualisation than terraced uniformity, with satellite dishes and replacement windows insensitive to the original design. A few examples of workers' housing have been preserved as museum displays, such as Joseph Parry's house in Merthyr Tydfil, the reconstructed terrace from Rhyd-y-Car at St Fagans, and rows at the National

Slate Museum in Llanberis and Blaenavon Ironworks.

Terraced housing can be found in all coal-mining areas of the United Kingdom and in most working-class areas. There isn't anything uniquely Welsh about the designs, yet the terraces of Wales feel particularly Welsh in their use of local stone and detailing. It would be hard to imagine Wales without them; in fact the valleys wouldn't be the valleys without them. The humble terraced home has certainly played its part in building the Wales we know today by housing the people who created the industry that supported the economy of our nation.

Tredegar House

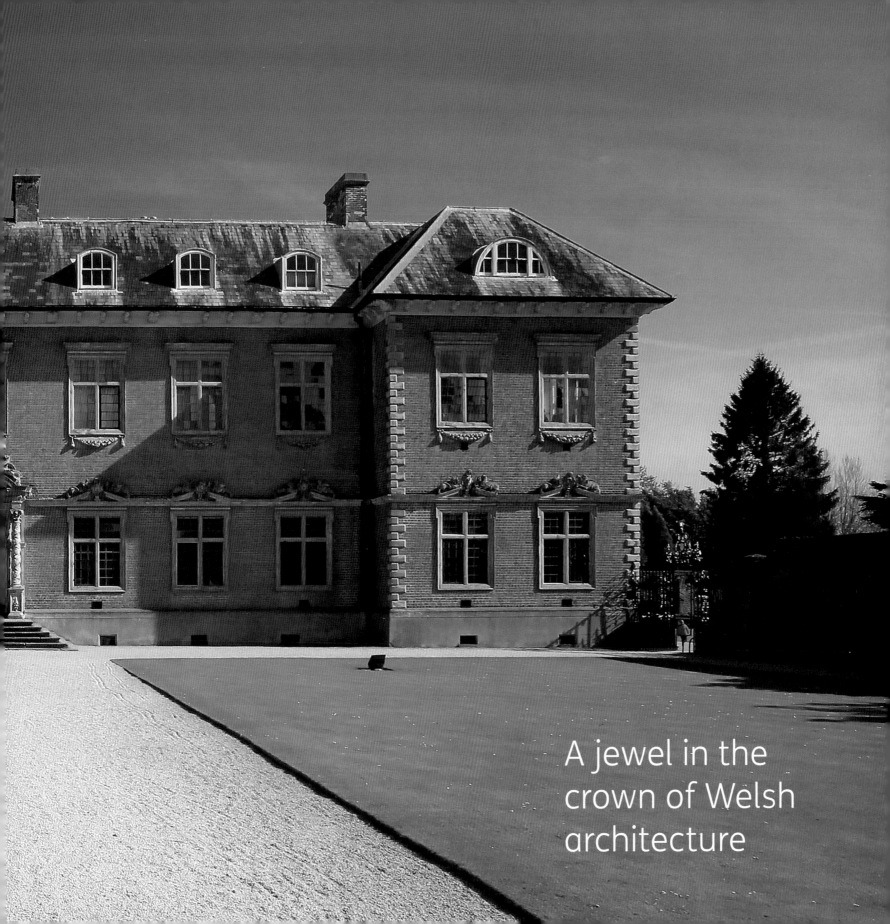

A jewel in the
crown of Welsh
architecture

Tredegar House

People: Sir William Morgan (c.1640-1680).

Place: Tredegar House, home to the Morgan dynasty of south-east Wales and now a visitor attraction managed by the National Trust. The grandest and most exuberant country house in Monmouthshire and one of the outstanding houses of the Restoration period in the whole of Britain, Tredegar House was the ancestral seat of the Morgan family.

Event: The first and also the most impressive Restoration house to be built in Wales.

A jewel in the crown of Welsh architecture and one of Britain's finest seventeenth-century buildings, Tredegar House was rebuilt on a lavish scale between 1664 and 1672, with work commissioned by Sir William Morgan incorporating the original sub-medieval house. The Morgan dynasty had residences over much of south-east Wales, with principal family members based at Machen, Tredegar and Ruperra during the opening years of the seventeenth century. Clearly influenced by the work of Inigo Jones, Tredegar House retains many exquisite Restoration rooms as well as an impressive stable block and an outstanding orangery set amongst formal gardens.

The search for attribution has been a continuous, underlying topic in the study of Welsh country houses during the last fifty years. Howard Colvin's article for *Architectural History* in 1982 carefully dissected the plan, structure and decoration of Tredegar House, Newport, in order to identify the designer. Tree ring dating has dated the primary timbers of the sub-medieval house to a felling date range of 1544-74. The mid-sixteenth century house was partially reconstructed following a fire, and had a felling date range of 1624-54. The main building had felling dates of winter 1666/67, winter 1670/71 and winter 1671/72.

Colvin suggests, on the basis of the plan and elevation, that the most likely 'artisan architect' was Roger or William Hurlbutt, whose work at Maiden Bradley, Wiltshire, he cited as being comparable. Richard Suggett, however, suggests that Tredegar has closer stylistic parallels with Sir Roger Pratt's Clarendon House (built 1664-67), a conclusion that is also supported by tree-ring dating. Tredegar House is unique in Wales in terms of its scale, form and decoration. It is an evolutionary house even though the Restoration front masks the earlier structures.

In 1951 the Morgans left Tredegar, never to return, and the house was used as a Roman Catholic boarding school until it was purchased by the local authority in 1971. Many years have since been spent painstakingly restoring the house and gardens. The collections were slowly reassembled, particularly through the fundraising support of the Friends of Tredegar House. After many years of negotiations, in 2012 Newport Council signed a fifty-year lease to the National Trust to take on the management of the house and its ninety acres of gardens and park. Under National Trust rebranding, Tredegar is open to the public as a major

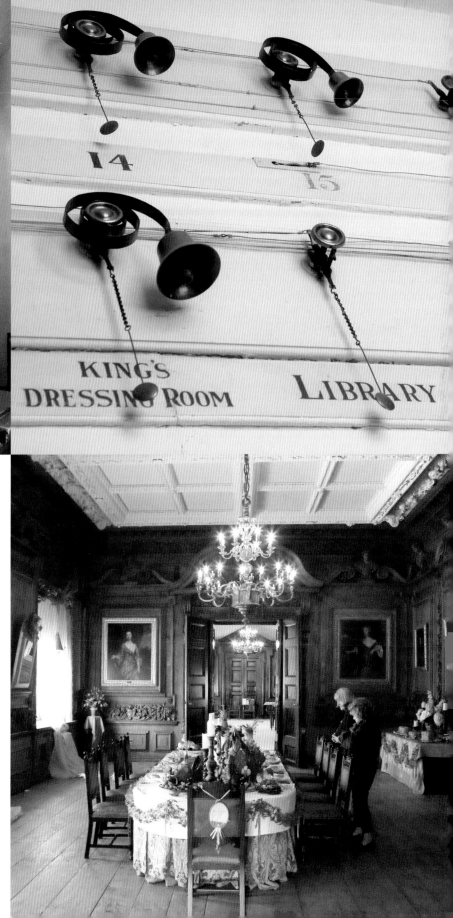

tourist attraction in south Wales and is one of the Trust's flagship properties in south-east Wales. Unlike in England, the National Trust has relatively few great houses in Wales, with most of their property being coast and countryside. Tredegar was a decisive move in terms of long-term Trust agenda, given most of the population of Wales can be found around Cardiff, Newport and the Valleys. They needed somewhere for the people to visit, and Tredegar has so far proven extremely popular.

Port Talbot
Steelworks

It is known locally, somewhat lovingly, as Isengard, the 'iron fortress' from Lord of the Rings

Port Talbot Steelworks

People: Christopher Rice Mansel Talbot (1803-1890) and his daughter Emily Charlotte (1840-1918).

Place: Formerly the Margam Iron and Steel Works and owned by Tata Steel, Port Talbot remains the largest of Britain's three principle steelworks.

Event: The longest integrated steelworks in Europe, during the 1960s Port Talbot was the largest single employer in Wales, employing over 18,000 people.

Port Talbot Steelworks is one of the longest structures in Europe and, for a time, was one of Wales' largest employers. The steelworks are a daunting site and sight, impressive in massing, depressing in detail, essential for employment and industry. The whole site is made up of several plants, which have been successfully developed and enlarged since the early twentieth century. It is known locally, somewhat lovingly, as Isengard, the 'iron fortress' from *Lord of the Rings*, as it looms over the coastal strip past the Margam estate. Had the conceptual artist for the *Lord of the Rings* film trilogy seen Port Talbot?

The area around Port Talbot has been industrialised since the late eighteenth century when a copperworks was established there in 1770. A dock was opened in 1839 and named after the Talbot family of Margam Castle, the local landowners and developers of the ironworks. Margam Abbey was a

Cistercian foundation, established in 1147. Following the dissolution of the monasteries in the mid-1530s, the former monastic lands came into possession of the Mansel family who, through female descent, became the Talbots. The industrial revolution was taken up with full gusto by the Talbots who owned the shoreline, together with the historic harbour for the River Afan's estuary. Coal mining was its first taste of organised industry and provided much revenue for developing the Margam estate.

The expansion of ports for import and export grew in conjunction with the improvement of roads and the resultant opening up of Wales. Turnpikes enabled communication between London and the more remote regions of Britain, and this no doubt hastened the transference of ideas more easily. These roads created an integral infrastructure for turning what were once distant and isolated areas into new territory ripe for expansion.

Christopher Rice Mansel Talbot had a keen eye for business, establishing an ironworks in 1831. Talbot's daughter, Emily Charlotte, continued her father's tradition of investing in heavy industry, further developing the port and its railway connections, in a bid to rival, perhaps even to supersede, Cardiff and Swansea. The Port Talbot Railway and Docks Company was incorporated in 1894, opening in 1897, to transfer raw materials from the valleys to the docks at Port Talbot. At its height, around three million tonnes of coal were being exported through the docks in the 1920s.

Steel was to overtake coal in terms of material fuelling the economy of Port Talbot. The original works were built between 1901 and 1905, and named in honour of Christopher Rice Mansel Talbot. These were enlarged in 1923 to become the Margam Iron and Steel Works. In 1952, the Steel Company of Wales completed the Abbey Works, erecting the largest integrated steelworks in Europe and employing 18,000 people, which went on to make it the largest single employer in Wales during the 1960s. A new deep-water harbour was opened in 1970 which allowed for an increase of vessels up to ten times in size. The Abbey Works, which occupies a site over a mile in length, is capable of producing up to five million tonnes of steel slab a year, and it is still the largest of Britain's three principal steelworks. The M4 skirts around the edge of the site, which provides a major landmark for visitors on their way to west Wales.

Christopher Rice Mansel Talbot had a keen eye for business, establishing ironworks in 1831

Tata Steel currently own the steelworks, and have a sister plant at Llanwern Works in Newport as part of a network of operations across 80 countries worldwide. Five thousand employees work at both Port Talbot and Llanwern, although recently announced job losses will soon adversely affect that figure. An integrated system is employed between the two sites with steel being rolled into strips at Port Talbot before a metallic coating is added at Llanwern to protect against corrosion. The main uses of steel are still in car manufacturing, with the market sector recording 34% use for automotive, 18% for the construction industry and the rest for general industry.

Community payback is now an important element of the work undertaken by Tata. In response to environmental performance, the Steel Gas Recovery scheme aims to capture waste gases and allow their re-use as a secondary fuel on site, rather than let them pollute the atmosphere. On a somewhat lighter note, *Top Gear* have used the Port Talbot steelworks a number of times to film, and director Terry Gilliam cited the Port Talbot Steelworks as an inspiration for his film *Brazil*.

Castell Coch

Romantic nineteenth-century interiors

If you are one of the richest men, or possibly the richest man, in the world you probably don't need to worry about whether you or another industrial magnate is the wealthier. You have enough money to do exactly whatever takes your fancy and, in the case of John Patrick Crichton-Stuart, third Marquess of Bute, this often meant indulging in his interest in medieval art and architecture. The architectural heritage of Wales is the richer for his contribution.

It is interesting that a man made rich by expanding Wales' coal and iron industry was, like many of his wealthy contemporaries, more interested in the pre-industrial era; its art, architecture and literature. As Wales moved towards the modern age with increasing urbanisation and industrialisation, many of the rich turned their interests to a time they perceived as being a 'golden age' in history, a period when life was good and simple, and buildings were beautiful. The Arts & Crafts movement and the pre-Raphaelite art movement would probably never have been sparked had Europe not seen significant industrialisation in the nineteenth century.

Many of the middle classes in the later nineteenth century chose homes that loosely reflected an understanding of Gothic design, and acres of suburban Cardiff homes were built with Gothic arches in their windows and doors and medieval-influenced tiling in their hallways and entrances. It's the same story in Aberystwyth and all the other towns that

Detail from the decoration in the Lady Bute's Bedroom.

were expanding in the third quarter of the nineteenth century. The 'billionaires' of their day such as the Marquess of Bute had the opportunity to go several steps further, and build their own replica castles. In Wales he notably remodelled Cardiff Castle with lavish Gothic-revival interiors designed by art architect William Burges.

Much smaller than Cardiff Castle is Bute's rebuilding of Castell Coch near Tongwynlais. Unlike Cardiff it represents a virtually new building, and a purer version of the Bute/Burges partnership. The Marquess had met Burges in 1865 in Scotland when the architect was already known as an accomplished 'medieval' architect designer responsible for Saint Fin Barre's Cathedral in Cork. Burges, who never married, was considered

Castell Coch

People: John Patrick Crichton-Stuart, third Marquess of Bute (1847-1900), patron, William Burges (1827-1881), architect.

Place: A small, mostly Victorian 'hunting lodge' castle built in a romantic revival style on older foundations above Tongwynlais, Cardiff.

Event: With Cardiff Castle, Castell Coch represents the pinnacle of the romantic and Gothic revival styles that came to characterise the new urban architecture of Cardiff. It is also symbolic of the immense wealth created by the coalfields of south-west Wales, and an industrial era 'call' back to pre-industrial design.

The painted ceiling in the Drawing Room.

by his contemporaries to be eccentric, over-indulgent and flamboyant, once commenting that 'good art is far too rare and far too precious ever to be cheap'. Under Bute's patronage he developed into Britain's greatest Gothic-revival architect designer.

However, Bute provided much more than just a blank cheque for the Cardiff Castle and Castell Coch projects: he had a genuine interest in medieval antiquarianism and scholarship himself.

Together the pair remodelled Cardiff Castle and work began in 1875 to build on the heavily ruined remains of Castell Coch using many of the same craftsmen and builders.

Castell Coch was to be 'a country residence for occasional occupation in the summer'. Burges rebuilt the castle around the motte, comprising a shell-wall, a projecting circular tower, a gatehouse and a square hall above an undercroft. Although Burges' building was clearly informed by the ruined foundations of Castell Coch, he generally

used his imagination in modelling the structure. Today the decorative towers appear vaguely continental as they rise from the beech forest planted around the site.

By 1879 the structure was complete, and the immense task of creating the highly decorative interiors commenced. Burges died in 1881, though his colleagues completed the project according to his plans, working for another decade. The interiors of Castell Cochand as Cardiff Castle inspire awe, with their heavily detailed decorated, frescoed, painted and lacquered surfaces. Behind all this medieval revival were discreet modern heating and plumbing systems that were state of the art in their day. The decoration and ornament intoxicates with its detail; each room causes the viewer to pause and stare, marvelling at the intricacy of the Gothic-revival decoration, the portraits, and the commissioned furniture that remains intact. Hours can be lost moving from room to room interpreting the allegories in the frescoes and gazing at the sheer wealth of the jewel-like decoration. Lady Bute's bedroom at the top of one of the three towers is a particular delight, being Moorish in design under an Arabic dome, and with an immense bed painted red and gold with crystal balls attached as bedknobs. You feel that Guinevere may have just left the room.

Despite having created one of the most decorative and beautiful interiors of nineteenth-century Britain, the Marquess of Bute visited infrequently, having a number of larger and more comfortable homes, not least Cardiff Castle and the immense Mount Stuart house in Scotland (designed by R. R. Anderson, also in the Gothic-revival style). Castell Coch was a luxury retreat to use for occasional picnics and short stays, being too far from Cardiff for regular use. The Marquess took great pride in his patronage of restoration and new architectural projects across Britain, and contributed to many chapels, castles, abbeys, universities and palace projects. Most follow the Gothic-revival style seen at Castell Coch. In 1950 the fifth Marquess of Bute handed the little-used castle into state care, and it is currently managed by

Cadw, Wales' heritage agency.

Castell Coch could easily have been a disaster in terms of design and architecture. Unlimited budgets are wonderful things, but they don't always lead to successful design. Yet Burges at Castell Coch created something different, something more than a medieval replica. It isn't in fact a replica at all, it is a building heavily informed by medieval European design but it actually reflects late nineteenth-century interests of romance and a re-reading of history. It is also a delight to visit in ways that original medieval castles aren't; here is a completely wondrous interior, marvellous at every turn.

Castell Coch and the similarly decorative revamp of Cardiff Castle are among the finest nineteenth-century interiors in

Britain, and indeed Europe. They reflect fear of the industrial as the world was changing, and the desire to return to a simpler, stress-free life. More than a century later we've yet to escape that desire to seek simplicity in historic periods as a salve to modern day life.

**Above left: The central courtyard.
Above right: A window seat in the Banqueting Hall.**

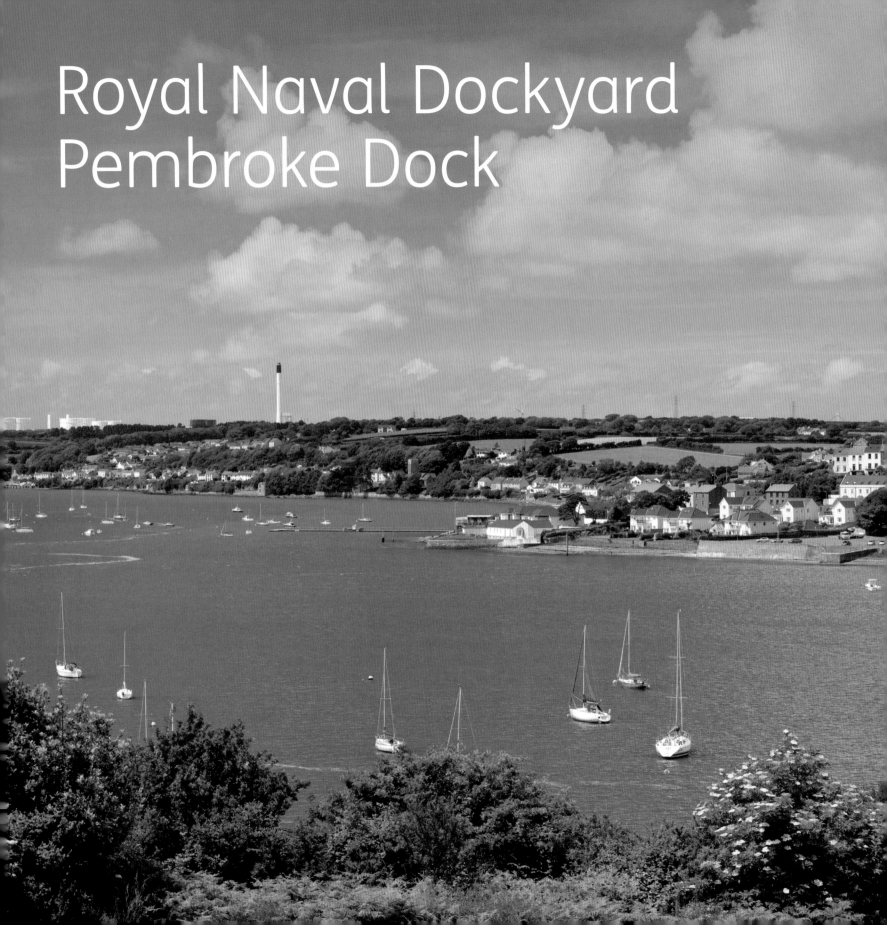

Royal Naval Dockyard
Pembroke Dock

Royal Naval Dockyard

People: The creation of the docks formed a new community based around the industry of shipping.

Place: 'Britannia Rules the Waves' – Pembroke Dock was part of a series of strategic military and mercantile ports along the coast of Britain, playing an important role in terms of defence and economy.

Event: During World War Two, the docks housed the largest operation of flying boats in the world. In 1979, the *Millennium Falcon*, a full scale spaceship, was built at the dock for Star Wars' *The Empire Strikes Back!*

Pembroke Dock helped build the economy of Wales during the eighteenth century. The lovely streets of Georgian naval buildings belie the industry and military might that once passed through these historic docks. Milford Haven had always been a sheltered harbour and a Naval report from 1758 recommended the erection of a dockyard. However, it was not until 1814, the height of the Napoleonic wars, that the Royal Navy dockyard was formally established, whereupon the first orders were placed

for a seventy-four gun battleship and four frigates. Pembroke Dock then became the first Royal Dockyard to be created purely for shipbuilding.

As the dock grew in importance, the need to militarise and defend the town grew. Defensible barracks and Martello towers of Portland stone were created in the 1850s to hold a garrison.

The dock continued to be active until the end of World War One and was sporadically used until its permanent closure in 1947. The last Pembroke-built frigate in use was the *HMS Inconstant* which ended its life in a breaker's yard in 1956. Even though it did not continue as an active dockyard, it retained a Queen's Harbour Master until 2008, being one of the last five dockyards to keep this post into the twenty-first century.

Many of the dock's buildings slowly fell into dereliction during the twentieth century as mass unemployment followed the closure of the Naval Dockyard. Some are very stately with the Master Surgeon's house being a prime example of one which could pass for a town house in Bath. Many have had a chequered history, such as the former home of the Captain Superintendent of the dockyard, built in

1832–4, and designed by Fox, Henderson and Co of Birmingham. This company famously erected Crystal Palace in 1851. The Captain Superintendent's house and office was recorded by *The Welshman* to have cost £2,867. Like most of the dock buildings, it was constructed out of tooled, grey squared limestone. During the 1930s, the building was used as an Officers' and Sergeants' Mess for the RAF and, in the 1960s, it opened as a hotel which had great success with travellers en-route for the Irish ferry. This closed several years ago and the building has been empty ever since.

Pembrokeshire County Council agreed in 2005 that they would issue a Compulsory Purchase Order for the building if a partner came forward to develop the site, as the owner had not complied with a previous Repairs Notice. However, during the early hours of 8th August 2006 the hotel was set ablaze; fire crews quickly arrived on the scene but the roof and upper floors had come crashing down. There were fears that a night watchman was trapped inside but luckily he had been working elsewhere when the hotel caught fire. The building has since been restored as part of the wider regeneration of the historic docklands setting, with the elegant

dockyard chapel (1831), market (1826) and 1851 Martello tower all having been restored as well.

Pembroke Dock not only contributed to the military might of Britain during the nineteenth century, but also to the economy of Wales. Two hundred and sixty-three vessels were built for the Royal Navy at Pembroke Dock, and during World War Two it housed the RAF's largest operational flying boat base. The shipbuilding and military operations created great wealth within the locality, providing jobs, commerce, and a community. Schools, chapels, institutes and public houses all emerged as people flocked to live within the confines of the docks. Pembroke Dock became world-famous for its shipbuilding, of which very little unfortunately survives today.

Kinmel Hall

Kinmel - sketch by the Hon.ble Mrs Mostyn (née Monk) - about 1860 - (Vaux family)

Kinmel Hall

People: The Hughes family; Samuel Wyatt (1737-1807), architect; Thomas Hopper (1776-1856), architect; William Eden Nesfield (1835-1888), architect.

Place: Nesfield's Kinmel became the largest private house in Wales, palatial in scale and reminiscent of the Palace of Versailles and Hampton Court Palace. It was also reputedly a 'Calendar House' with 365 rooms.

Event: The wealth of the copper boom from Parys Mountain threw the provincial Hughes family into the glare of eighteenth-century Britain. They went from being Anglesey curates and farmers to one of the richest families in Wales.

Copper was one of Wales' greatest exports in the eighteenth century and the profits were ploughed back into architectural patronage and cultural pursuits. During this period Wales was certainly no cultural backwater but perhaps would be better viewed as 'cosmopolitan Cymru'. The Welsh gentry employed some of Britain's greatest architects and interior designers, making the country homes of Wales treasure houses of a nation's story.

The Hugheses of Anglesey became incredibly rich due to their part ownership of Parys Mountain. In pursuit of subsequent gentry status, the Reverend Edward Hughes (1738-1815) purchased the historic Kinmel estate in 1786. There have been five mansions in and around the site of Kinmel, the first built by the

William Lewis Hughes, Lord Dinorben, was the fun-loving friend of royalty, who enjoyed great popularity in north Wales during his lifetime.

Lloyd family who, by marriage, passed the estate to the Hollands. During the Civil War, the house was held for Cromwell, who reputedly paid a visit there.

Eminently fashionable, Samuel Wyatt designed a Grecian villa a few hundred yards from the old house and Hughes commissioned Gillows and Co. to furnish the new house. Gillows was one of the most fashionable furniture makers of the period and part of the collection that was once at Kinmel can be seen on display at the Victoria and Albert Museum. In 1805, a whole suite of furniture was purchased for the drawing room at Kinmel in the most fashionable Regency style, with French Empire-inspired lions, sphinxes and leopards, causing one of the Hughes family to write: 'I do flatter myself that

your two rooms will be the neatest and most tasteful in your neighbourhood.'

William Lewis Hughes (1767-1852), later Lord Dinorben, inherited Kinmel from his father in 1815 and continued the patronage of Gillows, making the interiors even more sumptuous. The great and the good of the courts of George IV and William IV came to north Wales to stay at Kinmel with Dinorben. Tragedy struck in 1841 when Wyatt's house was gutted by fire. Fortunately, the family and furniture were evacuated but only the main walls and a portion of the offices survived. Thomas Hopper, who had been previously employed at Penrhyn Castle and Bryn Bras Castle, was appointed to raise the new Kinmel from the ruins of the old. Hopper literally encased the new Kinmel around

the walls of the Wyatt house.

Another generation later, the wealth and flamboyance of Hugh Robert Hughes (nicknamed HRH) called for another rebuilding of Kinmel, this time it was to be inspired by the splendours of Versailles and Hampton Court Palace. Between 1871 and 1876, William Eden Nesfield created a calendar house which reputedly contained 365 rooms, making Kinmel the largest private house in Wales. It was truly vast and palatial, and built to impress.

The sheer scale of Kinmel was its greatest attraction, but also its greatest downfall. After World War One, such massive builds became unworkable and the house ceased to be a private home, and was leased for various uses such as a Rheuma Spa and a girls' school. In 1975 the house was devastated by fire but this was mainly restricted to the roof and service areas, so the main rooms survived relatively unscathed. The house and estate were purchased back by members of the original family who sought out possibilities, including demolition for the damaged buildings. However, they were approached by a local businessman who offered to reinstate the house and turn it into a Christian conference centre. A 999-year lease was prepared with the first ninety-nine years at peppercorn rent with the proviso that the façades were restored. Work was spread out over several years with the aid of Welsh Office grants and bank loans thus enabling various parts of the house to open for use.

Today, after several failed reboots in the 2000s, it stands empty. Wouldn't it make a great Welsh National Portrait Gallery? It would be very in keeping with the ethos of arts collections amassed by the Hughes family with the wealth from Parys Mountain. North Wales needs a national cultural institution and Kinmel has enough wall-space to house the great wealth of paintings currently in store at St Fagans and the National Library of Wales.

Right, middle: The golden wedding anniversary of Hugh Robert Hughes and his wife, Lady Florentia.

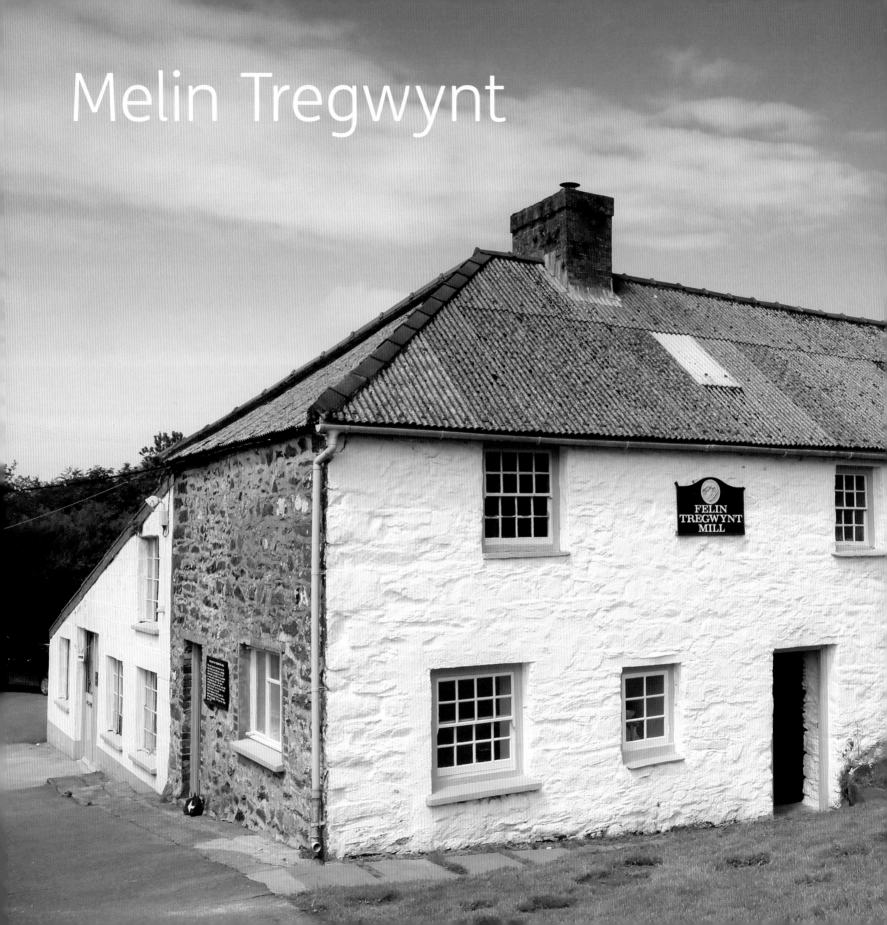

Melin Tregwynt

Melin Tregwynt isn't in itself a building that built Wales, but it is an interesting surviving representative of a once-great industry that did

The woollen industry in Wales may have declined in the second half of the twentieth century but for centuries it was an essential part of the rural economy. In fact, in the medieval period it could be described as the backbone of the Welsh economy, pioneered by the Cistercian monasteries that held huge swathes of land. In the early days wool was a more dependable source of income than land as crops could be burned but sheep were 'portable' and could be sold or hidden. Economically they were more 'liquid' than land. A significant wool trade developed between the producers in Wales and the markets in England and on the continent, and much of Wales' wealth derived from this source.

Today, there remain more sheep than people in Wales, although most are kept for the meat industry now that wool prices are low. Poor land that isn't readily suitable for arable farming is often better used as grazing for sheep, and whole valleys of buildings, particularly in the Brecon Beacons, owe their existence to

Melin Tregwynt

People: The Griffiths family of Melin Tregwynt, including Eifion Griffiths, present day partner/manager.

Place: A small vernacular estate woollen mill near the village of Castlemorris in north Pembrokeshire.

Event: Selected as typical of one of the hundreds of small woollen mills that formed the backbone of the significant Welsh woollen industry.

the boom in Welsh wool and flannel prices in the Tudor period. Before we started importing cotton, linen and artificially produced textiles, wool was a valuable and essential commodity which Wales could produce with ease.

Melin Tregwynt isn't, in itself, a building that built Wales, but it is an interesting representative of a once-great industry that did. South-west Wales in particular has a rich tradition of water-powered mills along the Teifi valley for grinding grain, fulling wool, and powering the looms that produced cloth. The heritage of the industry is evident in the names of homes in many villages in Carmarthenshire and Ceredigion, with Melin Uchaf, Melin Ganol, and Melin Isaf (Upper Mill, Middle Mill and Lower Mill) often standing just a few hundred metres apart.

Melin Tregwynt is smaller than many of the large nineteenth-century loom mills of Carmarthenshire and Ceredigion and is slightly earlier in its structure, having been built in the late eighteenth century. It has the look of one of the small 'parish' or estate mills seen across the three counties of Dyfed; in this case the estate being Tregwynt which originally owned a huge swathe of land from Fishguard to Mathry and which funded a mill on the site since the seventeenth century. The original mill was for grinding corn, converted later into a fulling mill where the wheel would drive the hammers that beat the woollen cloth. The heavy use of these corn and fulling mills, not to mention their riverside locations, explains why they were so frequently rebuilt, with some being literally shaken apart. Many of the west Wales mills stand on the site of mills of the 1600s, yet very few have any standing structure that date before 1750.

The third transformation of Dyffryn Mill at Tregwynt was to power the carding machines and looms that would weave the cloth that the mill is famous for today. Since that conversion, the water wheel has been retired and fast rapier looms powered by electricity now replace the flying shuttle looms. Anyone with an interest in hand or shuttle looms has to take a trip to the excellent Welsh Woollen Museum at Drefach Felindre.

The small-paned Georgian sash windows, limewashed walls and use of local colouring on the carpentry gives Melin Tregwynt a charming vernacular feel. Visitors enjoy their visits, but nothing has been contrived for tourism here, it's just that we've lost so many of these vernacular buildings that on the occasion we see one in good original order, with limewash sparkling and windows in charming blue, we assume it's probably something touristic. In fact the first shop for tourists opened at the site in the 1950s, when the Griffiths family who'd been running the mill since 1912 saw the opportunity to sell direct to the public. They opened other shops in the 1960s and 1970s selling their Welsh tapestry cloth direct to holidaymakers. Welsh 'carthen' designs, in often brilliant colours, were having a revival at the time, but the remarkable thing is that the mill has continued to thrive despite the general decline in the industry in the final quarter

of the twentieth century.

This small mill has moved with the times, producing contemporary designs, several of which have become so popular in the homes of the Welsh as to be instantly recognisable as Melin Tregwynt. They've also been successful in partnerships with international fashion houses, producing woollen cloth for some of the biggest names. Today about a third of their production is sold as export. The business markets the heritage of the mill and the Griffiths family that run it, and produces contemporary interpretations of traditional designs as well as historical reproduction cloth alongside modern patterns. Their textiles have become a symbol of Welsh craft production. Melin Tregwynt has become a brand and so they've managed to survive while many have disappeared. They aren't just selling quality woollen goods; they're selling the story of one of the last working woollen mills in rural Wales. People buy a blanket or throw or cushions from Melin Tregwynt because they're handsome products, but also because they symbolise the once great tradition of the Welsh looms.

During the last century our use of woollen fabrics has changed. We no longer tend to use blankets as the main form of bedding and today we consider the products of such mills as luxury 'artisan' products to be given as wedding gifts or special presents. What hasn't changed is the term 'Welsh wool' that still signifies quality production, as much now as it has done for many centuries. A little design inspiration is what it has taken to ensure that our great tradition will continue for years to come.

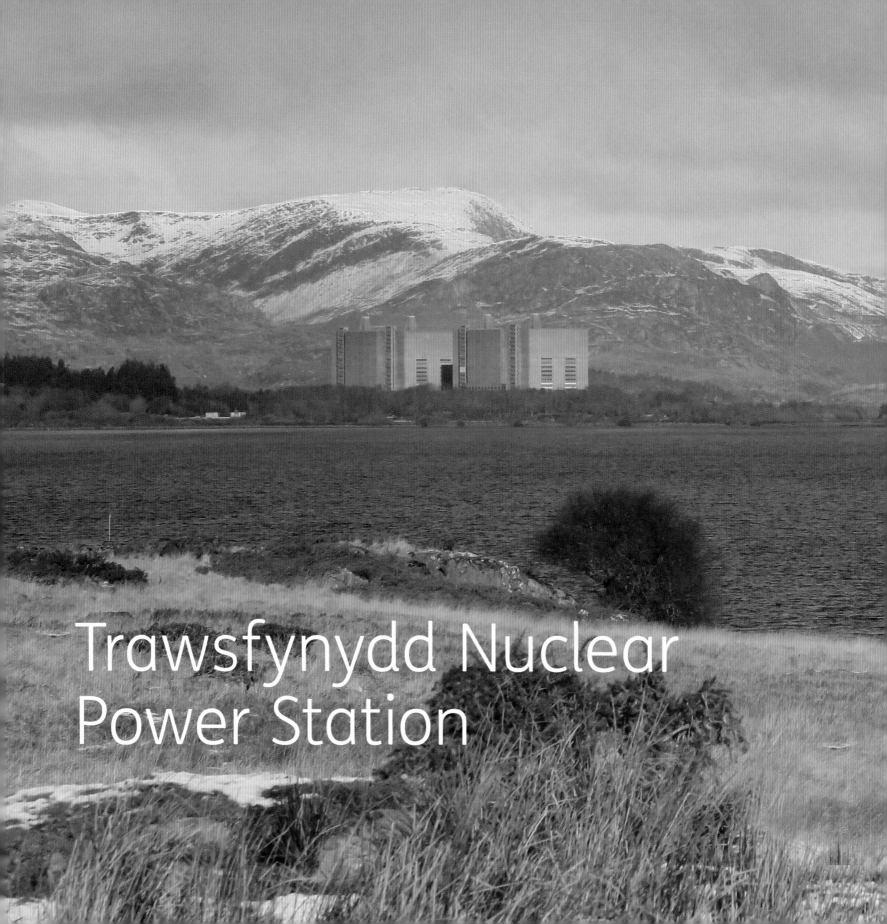

Trawsfynydd Nuclear
Power Station

Nuclear power, however controversial, has played its part in building the economy of Wales. It exported energy across the national grid and played a key role in supporting a nation. The numbers of jobs created during the process of building, running, and decommissioning the power station has so far sustained a community of workers for over fifty years. These people, both local and newcomers, entered a new way of life in the shadow of this modernist cathedral of twentieth-century technology.

The starkness and massing of the main building contrasts against the long, open vistas of the upland location

Trawsfynydd Nuclear Power Station

People: Designed by Sir Basil Spence (1907-1976) with landscaping by designer and garden architect, Sylvia Crowe (1901-1997).

Place: A foreboding and stark reminder of the Brutalist architecture of the Modernist movement, in a startling juxtaposition with the natural drama of Snowdonia.

Event: A search for clean energy was fraught with the perils of nuclear meltdown and widespread devastation. Fortunately, this potential catastrophic event never occurred.

The starkness and massing of the main building contrasts with the long, open vistas of the upland location, reflecting a mirror image in the adjacent Llyn Trawsfynydd reservoir. There is something frighteningly beautiful about a power station which is so alien to its location; it is, without doubt, magnificent.

The 1920s reservoir had been constructed to provide water for a hydro-electric power station at Maentwrog, which boasted the ability to supply the whole of north Wales' demand for electricity. A good, early example of going green. Construction of the nuclear power station began in 1959 at a cost of £103 million, to the design of Sir Basil Spence, out of reinforced concrete, with the twin reactor buildings reaching 180 feet in height. Spence knew that its use as nuclear power station was transitional, time-limited and that it would one day probably be ruined.

Comparisons can be drawn with Spence's radical Coventry Cathedral, which preceded Trawsfynydd by three years. Both buildings represent a forging of a

new British post-war identity which linked the past and present. It was truly and utterly confident, strident in its assertion of modernity. At Coventry, the medieval cathedral ruined by bombing during World War Two was itself retained as a garden of remembrance alongside the new structure, while at Trawsfynydd, the timeless, rugged outline of the surrounding mountains serves a similar purpose through its contrast with the futuristic structure of the power station. Sylvia Crowe softened the blow of the extensive building works by linking the twin buildings to their situation within Snowdonia national park.

The nuclear power station contained two Magnox reactors which could supply 470 megawatts in total. It was the first inland nuclear power station to be built in Britain and was decommissioned in the early 1990s. Opinion has been divided on the future of the site, with detractors wishing for it to be removed entirely. Others, more interestingly, have called for Spence's work to be saved, calling it a

'triumph of modernist architecture'. Some locals were angered by Westminster's decision to place the power station within their rural community, afraid of what the future would hold if a disaster occurred. Modernist architecture enthusiasts have been spurred to save the building from destruction, doubly so after the demolition of the Dunlop Semtex rubber factory at Brynmawr in 2001.

Is it time to forgive and forget the baggage of the past and celebrate what we have got? Spence's architecture will remain for some time as the decommissioning process will take another hundred years to complete, so for the time being, Trawsfynydd will remain a feature of Snowdonia's upland landscape.

St. Madryn Parish Church

Pontcysyllte
Aqueduct

Pontcysyllte Aqueduct

People: Designed by Thomas Telford (1757-1834) and William Jessop (1745-1814), the foremost civil engineers of the period.

Place: Now a World Heritage Site, the aqueduct was one of the great building feats of early nineteenth-century Britain.

Event: It is the longest and highest aqueduct in Britain, a physical display of Georgian confidence in economy and advanced construction techniques.

The years 1780 to 1914 were some of the most radical in terms of building and landscape transformation, with areas such as north-east Wales and the South Wales Valleys changing dramatically through industrialisation. Transport was the key to good industry, acting as the proverbial artery of a successful nation. Canals were the super highways of the early nineteenth century, allowing the relatively speedy transfer of goods between locations. The industrial revolution demanded an economical and reliable way to transport large amounts of goods over large distances effectively. Many of the canals crossed terrain that was not flat, so in the fashion of the Romans, aqueducts were a necessary part of a route which achieved the shortest, straightest distance possible. But even among aqueducts, Pontcysyllte is exceptional – it is the longest and highest in Britain.

As Wales was becoming a tourist destination during the late eighteenth century it was also being chosen as a home by many new wealthy entrepreneurial families, who either came with money, or based themselves near to their sources of income. The exploitation of mineral resources was fully realised by the Industrial Revolution in Wales, a movement greatly stimulated by the requirements, particularly for iron, of the Napoleonic wars. The chief areas of this expansion were the coal and iron districts of Monmouthshire and Glamorgan, along with the smaller scale coal, iron, and lead works of Flintshire and Denbighshire and the slate quarries of Gwynedd.

Scottish civil engineer and architect Thomas Telford was the designer of the aqueduct. Telford's work was primarily in Shropshire, under the patronage of William Pulteney. As county surveyor for Shropshire, bridges were one of the main structures for which Telford had responsibility, building forty within the county. His reputation for reliable and tested works became well-known, and he was appointed in 1793 to manage the construction of the Ellesmere Canal which linked the industrial sites of Wrexham with Ellesmere, Cheshire and Chester. It connected inland areas via a water network that led directly to the River Mersey and the sea. One of the most magnificent achievements of this new canal system was the Pontcysyllte Aqueduct, spanning the Vale of Llangollen and the River Dee. It looms 126 feet above the valley floor, with a length of 1000 feet, on a series of nineteen brick arches, each with a massive 45 feet span. (The lime

Pontcysyllte is the longest and highest aqueduct in Britain

mortar mix was said to have contained the blood of oxen.) This was all achieved with the detailed planning by William Jessop, whose specific expertise on canal construction was utilised.

The cast-iron trough was filled with water for six months during construction to make sure it was watertight. The Plas Kynaston Foundry at nearby Cefn Mawr produced the castings for the trough, which William Hazledine banked his business on. If he hadn't got the contract he would have gone bust. Opening on 26 November 1805, at a cost of £47,000, the aqueduct forms part of a canal system which begins at the Horseshoe Falls and which today has been designated a UNESCO World Heritage Site. Another highlight of the site, also designed by Telford, is the Chirk Aqueduct built in 1801, again with the trough cast by Hazledine. It was the forerunner of Pontcysyllte, crossing the Ceiriog Valley, with ten spans of masonry arches.

As the railway overtook the canal, a viaduct was erected in 1846-8 and reconstructed in 1858 by Scottish engineer, Henry Robertson (1816-1888). Robertson first came to north Wales to assess the potential for the development of minerals in the Brymbo area for a Scottish bank. Following his assessment, the bank offered to lend him the capital to take part in exploiting the mines himself. Several other young Scotsmen joined him, and they formed the Brymbo Mineral Railway Company, which purchased the Brymbo Hall estate, including Brymbo ironworks.

On his election to parliament, he purchased a house in London and a country residence called Crogen, a house situated on the Dee between Bala and Corwen. Robertson also rebuilt Pale Hall, near Bala, in 1871, which was said to be Queen Victoria's favourite Welsh house. The Llangollen Canal, with all its aqueducts and tunnels, represents the aspirations of an industrialising nation, whose manipulation of the landscape and its resources reached its peak in north-east Wales.

Llanerchaeron

The country house of Llanerchaeron, just inland from pretty Aberaeron, is noted for having been largely rebuilt by John Nash, the eminent Georgian architect. Nash is highly regarded for his work at Buckingham Palace (surviving on the rear façade), the fanciful Brighton Pavilion, the now destroyed Hafod near Cwmystwyth, and much of the celebrated Regency architecture of London.

Nash remodelled this 'plas' in a classic Georgian style, but Llanerchaeron isn't a major piece of his work, being executed on a middling budget and before he became the favoured architect of the Prince Regent. If you look around west Wales in particular you'll find many examples of his simple classical designs, especially in the gentry estates of the Teifi valley. Probably more than a dozen Welsh country houses show his hand. Despite its celebrity architect, Llanerchaeron (known as Llanayron to Nash) is significant more as a typical Welsh gentry estate, which reflected an interest in self-sufficiency and new agricultural practices.

Nash remodelled the existing country house for William Lewis in 1794, and to all extents what you see at Llanerchaeron today appears as a new Georgian villa of that period. Closer inspection inside reveals surviving masonry from the earlier house which we assume to be the seventeenth-century 'Llanychayron'. Nash's work in a simple classical style shows great attention to symmetry, to the extent that 'blind' windows were installed to make the house appear perfectly balanced from the outside. Nash was more interested in external appearance than internal practicality, placing windows on even levels externally which didn't suit the internal arrangement that had to accommodate the differing floor levels of the earlier house. As in many Nash works of the period, the main entrance is placed away from the staircase, the major internal feature, so guests walked down a corridor and turned before they were given the 'reveal' of the double-leg cantilevered stone staircase, lit from above.

The house would have been modern and comfortable for its inhabitants, with large sash window glazing, ample fireplaces and rooms of a manageable size. There are no great galleries or vast ballrooms, and even in winter this would have been a pleasant place to stay. The Greek Doric porch, although perfectly fitting, was added after 1845, complementing a handsome classical villa with Venetian windows, limed in a gentle ochre colour as if to appear a sandy stone. It is attractive without being grand.

What makes Llanerchaeron worth of inclusion here is that is a very good example of a Welsh rural country estate. It isn't the largest, the most impressive, the most influential, but it is typical of the unpretentious architecture that the Welsh gentry were building in the Georgian period. It is also a great place to understand how the wealthy were trying to order the world in their estates in the late eighteenth and early nineteenth centuries. The house has an unusually well designed service courtyard attached and a remarkable 'model farm' just yards away, through the impressive walled gardens. Together these make Llanerchaeron a model of self-sufficiency.

The unpretentious architecture that the Welsh gentry were building in the Georgian period

Llanerchaeron

People: John Nash (1752–1835), architect.

Place: A small west Wales gentry estate, with a Georgian estate villa remodelled in the late eighteenth century, in the Aeron valley near Aberaeron.

Event: Chosen for being typical of the many small and medium-sized Welsh gentry rural estates that managed the landscapes of Wales for centuries. Llanerchaeron is particularly interesting for how the landlords brought the 'model farm' into the public domain of an estate visit.

The display of the home farm at Llanerchaeron is significant, as previously the farms of country estates were merely functional and not of any particular interest to the landlord. At Llanerchaeron the farm was central to the new arrangement, attractively designed with good space and construction.

The villa itself is of a manageable size with just four good bedrooms entered off a central lantern-lit vestibule and with charming elliptical service dressing rooms. Downstairs, the receptions are similarly ordered, and all is well connected to the service wing which is unusually well laid out around a courtyard with brewery, salting room, laundries, scullery etc. There is nothing incidental about the service rooms of this country house. Everything has its place at Llanerchaeron, yet it was clearly designed on a relatively modest budget. The house is stucco rather than dressed stone, there is little ostentation, and the decoration is handsome, if restrained. This is what Welsh gentry housing is all about.

Llanerchaeron tells us about gentry society in west Wales. Of middling size, Welsh country houses tended to be built with minimal ostentation. This is significant because we don't have to look too far east to see gentry houses so decorative as to appear entirely built for show. The relationship between the master and his staff is clear here; they're very much part of the story.

The estate is managed by the National Trust for Wales these days, but such country estates have a long history of welcoming visitors, and at Llanerchaeron they would likely have been given a tour of the farm to show how the owner was familiar with the most recent thinking in farming practice. Although it can't be denied that there was a class structure in rural Wales in the Georgian period, houses like Llanerchaeron show that there was more parity between people in west Wales than there was, say, in London or Liverpool. The gentry families were highly regarded by their tenants, and the feeling was one of mutual respect and tolerance. It is tempting to 'read into' estates like Llanerchaeron that in Wales things were done slightly differently; staff were respected, and self-sufficiency was a greater virtue than any vulgar display of wealth.

The Queen of the Welsh resorts

Llandudno Promenade

Llandudno Promenade

People: Without the Mostyn family, Llandudno as we know it would not exist. Generations of the Mostyn barons have loved and cared for the town which has been crowned Queen of the Welsh Resorts.

Place: Victorian Wales can still be experienced in what is one of Britain's most untouched historic seaside resorts. The great sweep of Llandudno promenade has remained virtually unchanged since its construction during the mid-nineteenth century.

Event: So many events have taken place in Llandudno it is difficult to choose. However, Lady Mostyn's female-only art gallery in 1902 is of particular global significance.

The Queen of the Welsh Resorts is the title given to one of Britain's best-planned nineteenth-century towns. It has retained so much of its character due to the diligence of Mostyn Estates who have worked hard to preserve the integrity of the town's Victorian structure, one of its main attractions. Tourism has been the fuel which has stoked the economy of the Welsh nation since the mid-eighteenth century. Ever since Lord Lyttleton (1709-

1773) stayed at the ancient house of Brynkir, Gwynedd in 1755 in order to ascend Snowdon, tourists have flocked to Wales.

This desire for visitors to holiday in Wales was perceptively detected by many of the Welsh gentry whose incomes were generally low, being reliant on agriculture and land rents. During the early nineteenth century, many of the great estates of Wales began to develop property for commercial use. Occupation around the area of Llandudno, specifically the Great Orme, is prehistoric. The copper mines were some of the most extensive in Britain, and with these natural resources, life prospered. By the 1840s the population of Llandudno was around 1000, with most working in the now much smaller copper mines, or in the fishing industry. In 1848, things began to change. An architect, Owen Williams, of Welsh descent but Liverpool-based, presented the then Lord Mostyn with radical plans to redevelop the sleepy fishing village. Rapid development took place over a twenty-year period between 1857 and 1877, under the supervision of Lord and Lady Mostyn.

The promenade is the centrepiece of the town, creating a dramatic sweep between the Great and Little Ormes, with a gridiron plan laid out for the streets behind. To connect the town with the views on top

Occupation around the area of Llandudno, specifically the Great Orme, is prehistoric

of the Great Orme, a funicular railway was erected between 1902 and 1903, climbing the steep slopes of the outcrop. Four of the original trams from 1902 are still in use today. An old quarry site was donated to the town by the Mostyns for pleasure gardens to commemorate Queen Victoria's Golden Jubilee, with outdoor theatres, miniature golf courses and picnic areas. To complete the Victorian wonderland, a pier was built to the side of the Orme, acting as a dock for sea-bound arrivals to the town from places such as Liverpool and the Isle of Man. The pier was built in 1878 at a length of 700 metres, and is the longest surviving pier in Wales (Rhyl Pier was slightly longer at 718 metres but was dismantled in 1973).

In 1902 Lady Augusta Mostyn (1830-1912) founded an important female-artist only gallery for Gwynedd Ladies' Arts Society (GLAS), seemingly one of the first in the world. She was someone not to be thwarted and, in retaliation for the Royal Cambrian Society's refusal to allow women members, she set up her own, thereby providing Wales' own contribution to women's liberation in the arts.

Unfortunately, the iconic sweep of Victorian town houses and hotel building line was destroyed by alterations to Venue Cymru in 2006. This architectural misdemeanour may have disrupted the famous frontage but the overall majesty of the town remains, attracting tourists from all over the globe. The

annual Victorian Extravaganza, held each May Day bank holiday weekend, allows Llandudno to relive its glorious nineteenth-century past again, even if only for a few days.

Hafodunos

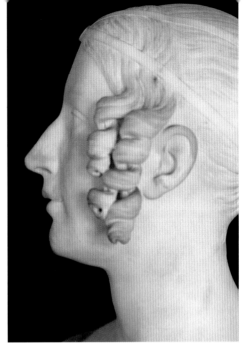

Hafodunos

People: Hafodunos was designed in the early 1860s by Sir George Gilbert Scott (1811- 1878) for Henry Robertson Sandbach (1807-1895) in memory of his first wife, Margaret Sandbach (1812-1852), and to house the sculptures of John Gibson (1790-1866).

Place: The Gothic Revival was an architectural movement that was to grip the imagination of the Welsh, and Hafodunos was one of the first private houses to be built in the Venetian style espoused by John Ruskin (1819-1900).

Event: The bohemian cultural circles of Victorian Britain would gather around the drawing rooms of Margaret Sandbach. This meeting of minds sparked a creative surge in the Welsh art scene during the middle decades of the nineteenth century.

Hafodunos, at Llangernyw near Abergele, earned its place amongst the most celebrated private homes in Wales for its hosting of bohemian, mid-Victorian literati. It was one of the first great Gothic constructions in Wales and set a precedent for the hundreds of houses, churches, chapels and civic buildings in the nineteenth century. The more playful yet correct Ruskinian Gothic expressed at Hafodunos had echoes of Venice and English Tudor mansions, mixing elements of the same form together in an asymmetrical composition. Not only was its architecture influential, but also its contents and landscaped gardens with its rare plant collections. These impacted on the way in which Wales evolved, and the vision of its owners can still be seen today, at the house itself but also within the nation's art collections. One of the statues from Hafodunos, Aurora, the Goddess of the Dawn, was used as the model for *Doctor Who's* 'Weeping Angels'.

The estate was bought in 1833 by a Liverpool merchant, Samuel Sandbach, a descendant of the original owners, the Lloyd family. Yet it was his son and daughter-in-law who were the principal occupants and it was under their influence that the new Hafodunos, Sir George Gilbert Scott's only example of domestic architecture in Wales, was built in the early 1860s to replace the seventeenth-century mansion.

Above left: Henry Robertson Sandbach and his second wife, Elizabeth Charlotte, commissioned the new Hafodunos to be designed by Sir George Gilbert Scott.

Above: The fragile beauty of Margaret Sandbach became the muse for Welsh sculptor, John Gibson, who preserved her beauty in marble long after her tragic death from breast cancer.

Henry Robertson Sandbach and wife Margaret (née Roscoe) were instrumental in turning a run-down and ramshackle parkland into one of the most efficient and beautiful estates of north Wales. Artists, writers and musicians flocked to this remote house, set high in the hills above the north Wales coast. Most famous of all of its visitors was the Welsh sculptor John Gibson, who became a close friend of the family and, as a result, the largest collection of his work was accumulated there. With him were people such as Penry Jones, Edward Lear and William Boxall. They all sought sanctuary in the beauty of house and landscape, but also in the frail, enigmatic beauty of Margaret Sandbach,

staying for months on end in a haze of creativity and mutual admiration.

This life of artistic endeavour was cut short in 1852 when Margaret died. A sculpture gallery was designed by Gibson for his favourite patron and muse, creating an almost mausoleum-like atmosphere at the house. His marbles were placed in reverence to the memory of the departed, and her poetry, plays and letters were read out loud by the mourning artists. It was through Margaret that Wales' greatest nineteenth-century sculptor found a home for his works in his native land. The Hafodunos marbles are now at the National Museum of Wales, Cardiff; Walker Art Gallery, Liverpool and the Royal

Academy, London.

From the main gates, one approaches the house along Gilbert Scott's new drive, winding and sensuous, with magnificent *Wellingtonia gigantea* along the right-hand side. At the main house, an *Escallonia macrantha* was reported in 1899 to cover over eighty square feet of terrace. The pre-Gilbert Scott landscape was planted between 1832 and 1852 under Margaret Sandbach's expert eye. Her mother had been a noted botanical painter whose work was published and highly valued in the 1820s. The collection of plants were advised by Sir William Jackson Hooker of Kew who was a close friend of William Roscoe

Most famous of all of its visitors was the Welsh sculptor John Gibson, who became a close friend of the family and as a result the largest collection of his work was accumulated there

which overlooked a miniature cascade and waterfall. Two stone bridges crossed the stream of the Nant Rhan-hir, being accessed from the terrace garden and forming a small circuit walk.

The valley walks were bordered by conifers, rhododendrons and many other evergreen plants, while on the valley floor were many varieties of *Pinus* and *Picea*. The *Coniferae* was always considered the true gem of the estate. Henry Robertson Sandbach had been a lover and planter of conifers, he was also an enthusiastic collector and raiser, with many of the finest and most unique specimens collected as cuttings, whilst he was on his travels, from trees in their natural habitats. The garden gained national prominence and it was the landscape to which the owners of Bodnant Garden turned. Only a few miles from what is now known as Wales' most famous garden, Hafodunos inspired Henry Davis Pochin and his gardener, Edward Milner to transform Bodnant.

Since leaving the hands of the Sandbach family in 1933, Hafodunos has had a variety of different functions as a girls' school, accountancy college and nursing home. A period of neglect ensued from 1993 onwards, but Cadw recognised the importance of the site, listing the house as Grade I and the gardens Grade II. Sadly the demise culminated in the destruction by arson of the interiors of the main house in October 2004. Previously, plans had been put forward to convert the house into a four-star Welsh boutique hotel with an enabling development of ninety Scandinavian-style wooden lodges in the grounds. It was suggested

MP, grandfather of Margaret Sandbach. Hooker corresponded with Henry and Margaret frequently between 1833 and 1852. Margaret never saw the garden reach its peak and maturity. In the 1890s there were Tea Roses on the terraces in front of the mansion, with several large plants of Fortune's Yellow, described as 'a most exquisitely beautiful variety, rarely seen doing so well in the open air'. On the terrace walls were many climbing plants which would have had to winter in

conservatories and greenhouses but had thrived in the north Wales climate.

At the bottom of the terrace flows a tributary of the River Elwy; along its banks and in other parts of the grounds are superb varieties of rhododendrons, and many other evergreen and deciduous shrubs. By the Edwardian period many of the Sikkim varieties had grown to sixteen feet high by twenty feet in diameter, and were backed up gracefully by conifers. Along the dingle, there was a rustic bridge

One of the statues from Hafodunos, Aurora, Goddess of the Dawn, was used as the model for *Doctor Who's* 'Weeping Angels'

that horticulture students could help restore the once magnificent gardens in conjunction with a charitable trust to oversee the restoration of the formal gardens and arboretum. It is currently under restoration as a private home by Dr. Richard Wood, and is frequently open to the public.

Right: Aurora, Goddess of the Dawn, immortalised in verse and sculpture by Margaret Sandbach and John Gibson.

Y Pafiliwn, National Eisteddfod of Wales

This week-long event moves from county to county each year in the first week of August and is a tremendous display of Welsh talent and culture

Y Pafiliwn

People: The people of Wales.

Place: An itinerant pavilion that accompanies the National Eisteddfod around Wales, with a new location each August.

Event: A week long festival of culture celebrating song, dance, drama, poetry and prose, as well as many other traditional crafts.

Left: Y Pafiliwn, Eisteddfod.

The cultural event of the year in Wales is the annual celebration of Yr Eisteddfod Genedlaethol Cymru – The National Eisteddfod of Wales. The week-long event moves each year from county to county, but wherever it takes place it offers a tremendous display of Welsh talent and culture. The Eisteddfod is a week-long series of competitions in the many traditional skills that Wales is proud of: singing, dancing, recitals as well as fine art, sculpture and architecture. You cannot visit the Eisteddfod without feeling great pride in the country; for many it is an essential part of the structure that makes Wales what it is. At the heart of the site is the main Pafiliwn or performance area, an immense, glorious marquee that is designed to be seen for miles around.

A pink Pafiliwn was first used for the National Eisteddfod in Swansea in 2006, causing quite a stir with its bold, cheerful colour. Since then the nation has quickly come to love the structure as an icon of the Eisteddfod and Welsh culture. Eisteddfodau can be traced back to Cardigan castle in 1176, but the modern national event we enjoy today was revived in 1861. In the early days the structure was termed the 'teyrnbabell', and the first one built for the 1861 event suffered an unfortunate fate, as told by the *North Wales Chronicle* on 24 August 1861:

'A spacious marquee with seats to contain 6000 people had been specially created …at an expense of several hundreds of pounds. But on Sunday last, during the prevalence of a strong westerly gale, the noble structure … was completely destroyed, and the whole expensive decorations exposed to the merciless storm. … However, the patriotic spirit of the promoters was not in the least daunted and they at once employed a large force to convey the materials to the Market Hall, where it was decided the meeting should take place.'

The design and structure of the pavilion continued to be of interest to the Welsh people and media, whether it be a wooden or canvas structure, as decided by the local committee. Many of the early pavilions were substantial in their construction, could house many thousands, and were lit by gas for evening performances. Every year there would be discussion in the local press about the quality of the internal decoration and how well the structure would stand up to the weather. Reporting on the 1888 pavilion at Wrexham, the *Western Mail* provided a detailed description of the structure:

'The pavilion in which the Eisteddfod is to be held is a really magnificent structure erected in the Grove Park at a cost of about £600. It is of circular form with a semi-circular wooden roof over the platform and reserved seats. It is, I am informed, expected to hold between 7000 and 9000…The pavilion is decorated with mottoes, and the 'Cof am a fu' tablets are fixed one on each side of the platform.'

In the early twentieth century, pavilions increased further in size to accommodate the swell in interest in the event, holding audiences of between twelve and fifteen thousand.

The modern day Pafiliwn has the same use as its predecessors. It is the tent

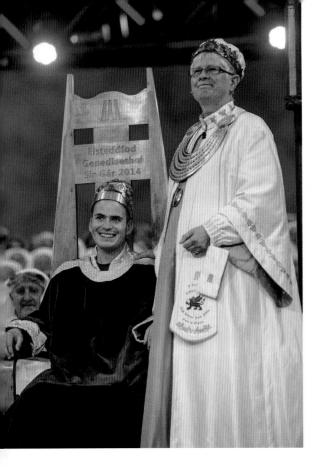

Above: Guto Dafydd being crowned at the National Eisteddfod of Wales, Llanelli 2014.

where most of the competitions are held, and where important ceremonies take place awarding the crown and chair for poetry. It has two rows of distinctive pinnacled tensile roof peaks that loosely remind us of a medieval romance. When fully extended it is the world's largest circus-style superstructure.

The famous pink tent which has been the focal point for activities since it's 2006 debut is hired from Dutch marquee specialists De Boer who refer to it as The Pink Galaxy. At the Eisteddfod it was built to seat two and a half thousand people, but this structure could also be contracted or extended according to demand. The Galaxy was the largest membrane tent in Europe when fully extended: although always sixty metres wide it could be extended up to 152 metres long, for up to 18,000 people or 4,500 seated. It could be erected in just a week, with the roof being ratcheted up the king poles inside each of the roof peaks (a sight in itself). The dark blue interior provided a warm and luxurious ambiance, perfect for lighting and filming as the whole event is broadcast by S4C. King posts supported the impressive roof that reached a height of over twenty metres and the posts were positioned to allow for good acoustics and unrestricted viewing from all angles. Used until 2015 the Galaxy provided the National Eisteddfod with a true identifiable icon. Whatever language you speak, there was no mistaking the significance of the week the 'big, pink tent' came to town.

It is, of course, expensive to hire Y Pafiliwn every year for the Eisteddfod, and money would be saved by using a fixed venue.

The whole event, attracting around 160,000 people costs about £3m to host. But to remain in one location would defeat the object of what the Eisteddfod is all about – for it brings Welsh culture and language to all areas of Wales, including those that no longer have any significant Welsh-speaking populations. Each Eisteddfod needs a centre, a hub, and the Pafiliwn provides that for the greatest celebration of Welsh culture in the world.

To say that the Eisteddfod Genedlaethol has helped build Wales is stating the obvious. This friendly and vibrant festival is the place where people come to celebrate being Welsh, to participate in Welsh culture and to feel a Welsh welcome, irrespective of their ability in the Welsh language. The Pafiliwn is a national stage for music, dance, singing and all types of culture. It is an arena where you will experience the finest skills in all these disciplines being demonstrated by exponents from every part of Wales; ostensibly in competition but also in a unique communal celebration of culture. Simply by attending you instantly feel part of the Welsh community, linked to the immense heritage of the Eisteddfod and the wider culture of Wales. Wales is probably guilty of not singing its own praise enough, but once a year, for a whole week, the Welsh rejoice in their culture and reconfirm their sense of nationhood in one large and wonderful tent.

Castell Brychan

Castell Brychan

People: David Jenkins (1848-1915), hymn writer, J. Saunders Lewis (1893-1985), dramatist and political activist, Cyngor Llyfrau Cymru / Welsh Books Council.

Place: A much-remodelled early Edwardian villa on a hillside overlooking the bay in Aberystwyth, showing gothic influences.

Event: As the home of Cyngor Llyfrau Cymru / Welsh Books Council, Castell Brychan is the home of Welsh publishing and literature, and an invaluable asset in preserving the culture of Wales in both languages.

If you look north up the steep hill that contains the town of Aberystwth in its bowl, you'll see a cream-painted stucco building with a small crenellated tower that is home to Cyngor Llyfrau Cymru, the Welsh Books Council. Castell Brychan deserves a place in the Buildings that Built Wales because of the work undertaken there to nourish the literature and cultural education of Wales and the Welsh language. Wales would undoubtedly be a poorer place without Cyngor Llyfrau and its work.

Castell Brychan itself is a solid, if unremarkable, building that reflects its history as a Catholic college of theology. There is a large gothic-inspired window lighting the gable of the council chamber (formerly the chapel) and stylised crenellations either side of the front gable and decorative tower at the side. Its chief delight is undoubtedly the panoramic vista of the town and bay below.

The house was originally built for Welsh composer and hymn writer David Jenkins sometime around the turn of the twentieth century. Jenkins, originally from Trecastle, moved in 1874 to study music under the great Joseph Parry at Aberystwyth University. From 1893 he started lecturing and eventually became a professor in 1910. Jenkins died in 1915 and by 1923 the 'castle' had been turned into St. Mary's College, where Saunders Lewis taught for a spell. The theological college radically extended the property, adding the substantial chapel wing to the right as you face the main elevation. The Welsh Books Council also extended it to the left after it became their headquarters, with perhaps a little less architectural finesse.

The conversion for Cyngor Llyfrau saw the chapel converted into the Council Chamber, retaining the high ceiling and stained glass windows. The snooker room became an exhibition space and now holds the permanent exhibition of children's books. Saunders Lewis's former seminar room became an office, and the design department converted one of the bathrooms into a darkroom, with the bath useful for washing the prints.

Founded in 1961, and funded by the Welsh government, Cyngor Llyfrau supports the publishing industry of Wales in both languages. It helps publishers with grants, editing, design, marketing and distribution, as well as promoting reading and literacy throughout the nation. The Welsh have always had a strong interest in literature in both languages, both poetry and prose, and it is no surprise that the highest cultural achievement in the country is to be awarded the crown for pryddest – poetry in free verse, and chair for awdl – poetry in strict metre, at the National Eisteddfod.

Today the Council employs up to fifty staff in the offices in Castell Brychan and the large distribution warehouse in Llanbadarn Fawr. The annual turnover of around £5million reflects the strength of the Welsh publishing industry with the support of the Council, and titles from Welsh publishers and of Welsh interest are distributed to around eight hundred outlets from as many as three hundred and fifty publishers. Three schools officers visit over five hundred schools each year and, together with three further sales representatives covering the retail trade, collect orders for stock valued in the millions. Grants are awarded to help publish material in Welsh and English (including this book), and have been particularly successful in supporting Welsh language material for children.

The Welsh publishing industry would undoubtedly be weaker without Cyngor Llyfrau, which supports authors, editors, designers and publishing houses. Even though the Welsh purchase many more books per head per year than their English neighbours, we still need the Council to support new and adventurous projects. The Council has helped Wales understand her own culture. It works to keep the Welsh language alive, and teaches those outside Wales about our wonderful nation.

Pont Trefechan

Pont Trefechan

People: Sir James Weeks Szlumper (1834-1926), civil engineer; Cymdeithas Yr Iaith Cymraeg (The Welsh Language Society); John Davies (1938-2015) Welsh historian and political activist; J. Saunders Lewis (1893-1985), dramatist and political activist.

Place: An 1886 re-building in stone of earlier bridges that cross the Rheidol at Aberystwyth. It is attractive without being architecturally remarkable.

Event: The site of a politically significant protest in 1963 when a small group of student protesters briefly blocked the bridge, closing the main coastal route of Wales. With hindsight we can see that this was an iconic moment in the fight to protect the Welsh language and raise national and international consciousness about Welsh culture.

Wales has many impressive bridges, some of which may have justified an entry in this selection by their beauty and structure alone, but the most significant bridge that 'built' modern Wales is probably a simple nineteenth-century structure crossing the Rheidol at Aberystwyth. Pont Trefechan is a handsome piece of engineering built in 1886 to the design of the delightfully-named Chief Surveyor of Aberystwyth, Sir James Weeks Szlumper. The river had been crossed since medieval times at this point, and Szlumper's design spans the

Rheidol in three broad arches where the John Nash bridge of 1797 had previously stood. The design is simple and attractive, but not exceptional.

Pont Trefechan is significant because of the events of 2 February 1963, when the bridge was closed by a short sit-down protest by members of Cymdeithas yr Iaith Gymraeg (the Welsh Language Society). By forcing the temporary closure of this bridge they effectively blocked the main north-south transport route along

the western seaboard of Wales, and thereby brought great attention to their cause. It was a simple, peaceful protest that showed that ordinary people could cause significant disruption with minimum effort.

Cymdeithas yr Iaith Gymraeg had been formed the previous year in Pontarddulais in response to a now famous radio lecture, Tynged yr Iaith / Fate of the Language, by playwright Saunders Lewis. The dramatist spoke out in response to the 1961 census

results which showed that the proportion of Welsh speakers had declined to only 26% of Wales' population. Something needed to be done and Cymdeithas, took the call to action.

Looking back from the twenty-first century it is easy to forget how, only half a century ago, the Welsh language was hardly seen on the buildings and streets of Wales. Chapel notice boards would be inscribed in Welsh, but all signage, paperwork, and anything formal, legal

It was a simple, peaceful protest that showed that ordinary people could cause significant disruption with minimum effort

or official was undertaken in the English language; a language that was the second-tongue for many. Cymdeithas sought to bring equality to the language of the people of Wales, and Trefechan was their first significant protest.

John Davies, the late, great historian of Wales was one of the organisers of the 1963 protest. In 2012 he recalled the events of the day:

'Members went to Pont Trefechan and sat down to block the traffic, a protest that was in no sense part of the original plan [plastering public buildings with posters and slogans]. That produced some dramatic pictures, especially that of Rhiannon Silyn Roberts knocked out by a car driver and lying supine in the snow. Some of the drivers who were stuck on the bridge began dragging the protesters away. Those dragged lay supine; the possibility of punch-ups was avoided, for the principle of non-violence was built into the movement from the beginning. Virtually all the leading British newspapers gave extensive coverage to the events, with the Guardian *providing a headline exulting in the fact that 'A Whole Town was Welshed On'. Saunders Lewis was delighted and sent a cheque for two guineas to the movement's non-existent account.'*

Thirty minutes of protest blocking a narrow bridge had no lasting impact on the transport links of Wales, but it has had an immense influence on the rights of Welsh speakers. Trefechan sparked in people a realisation that they could do something to reverse the decline in the Welsh language. As Cymdeithas grew in strength through the 1960s and 1970s as a direct action pressure group, so did the pride with which many Welsh speakers regarded their tongue. Methods of protest over the years have included sit downs, hunger strikes and occasionally break-ins. People have been arrested and even served time in prison for their protests, and this has attracted the media attention that has forced the Welsh and British authorities to change their stance.

Today there is no need to cross Pont Trefechan as you drive the north-south route in Wales, but if entering Aberystwyth it makes for a short and pleasant detour where one can pay pilgrimage to the events of that cold morning in 1963. As you cross the bridge you now enter a town whose essential character has been informed by, and to an extent formed from, those events. Today the commercial signage of Aberystwyth is largely bilingual, reflecting the language of the residents of the town. The road signs that guide you into the

centre will also be in Welsh first, another fruit of the labour of Cymdeithas.

On the streets of Aberystwyth, and despite a substantial population of students from outside Wales, you will hear the beautiful language of Wales being used in everyday life. The decline in the language of the 1961 census has been reversed, and the people of Aberystwyth proudly use and protect their tongue. Cymdeithas remains a campaigning body based in the town, and we can thank it for its influence in the 1993 Welsh Language Act as well as the establishment of the Welsh language TV channel S4C that started broadcasting in 1982. As the home of the National Library, the Welsh Books Council and other devolved national institutions, Aberystwyth has become an unofficial Welsh-language capital for Wales. Many of those students from the original protest have stayed locally and opened businesses in the area, providing a structure of bookshops and publishers that have also helped nourish the language. Aberystwyth is undoubtedly culturally richer today because that simple bridge was blocked for a short period in 1963, and so too is the whole of Wales.

Tŷ Mawr, Wybrnant

Tŷ Mawr, Wybrnant

People: William Morgan (1545-1604), Bishop of Llandaff and St Asaph; George Douglas Pennant (1836-1907), Second Baron Penrhyn.

Place: A much remodelled and restored Snowdonia House essentially of the late sixteenth and early seventeenth centuries, located near Penmachno in Snowdonia.

Event: Celebrated as the birthplace of Bishop William Morgan who is considered crucial in the story of the survival of the Welsh language through his translation of the Bible.

The drive to Tŷ Mawr, Wybrnant, is one of the most pleasant tourist routes in north Wales, winding gently through steep, dramatic and picturesque valleys. You have an impression that you are in the middle of nowhere, yet north Wales in Tudor times was an important place that would have felt far less remote than we may now imagine. Although Wales has seen a shift in power to the south since the Industrial Revolution, it used to be north Wales that was the better connected, wealthier, and more cosmopolitan. This is reflected in the wealth of good, early, fashionable buildings that were constructed in Snowdonia.

Tŷ Mawr, Wybrnant, usually referred to with its valley name attached as Tŷ Mawr, or Great House, is another of the buildings in this book that deserves inclusion both for architectural and historical merit. It is one of the best presented Snowdonian Tudor houses and it was also the birthplace of Bishop William Morgan, who first translated the full Bible into Welsh and who is therefore celebrated for his immense contribution to the survival of the language.

The house itself is a medium-sized, wealthy, upland farmhouse of the late Tudor period. At first glance it appears easier to 'read' than it actually is, as the building has been twice restored: once in 1888 by Lord Penrhyn to celebrate the tercentenary of Morgan's translation, and again a century later (including a new roof) by the National Trust for the quatercentenary. Today the house sits without limewash, in which it is likely to have been dressed, for much of its life.

It appears that the house was rebuilt during Bishop Morgan's lifetime and incorporated the remains of an earlier house. The two substantial chimneys (one now leaning) would have been a symbol of wealth in the late sixteenth century as many lived in properties with open hearths and smoke filtering through a roof louvre or thatch. The two chimneys would have told any passer-by that there was a fire for cooking and another for a private parlour or bed chamber: a new luxury for many. Inside is a wonderful flagged floor and modern post-and-panel partitions that probably reflect how it was during Bishop Morgan's day. You can see the base of a former cruck remaining in one of the walls, an echo of the previous life of the building as an open hall house. Replica oak mullion windows suggest how it may have been at the end of the sixteenth century. The house is dressed with a collection of early Welsh furniture and early copies of Morgan's Bibles as well as Bibles in other languages donated from around the world.

Bishop William Morgan was born at Tŷ Mawr on the Gwydir Castle estate. He attended St. John's College in Cambridge, graduating in 1568 and 1571 before commencing seven years of biblical studies including study of the Bible in Greek, Hebrew and Aramaic. Morgan was ordained in 1568 and by 1578 was vicar of Llanrhaeadr-ym-Mochnant where he produced his famous Bible translation. The first translation of the New Testament into Welsh had been published by William Salesbury in 1567, while Morgan was studying in Cambridge. He translated

the Old Testament in the 1580s and published it together with a revised version of Salesbury's New Testament in 1588. He went on to revise the text which included a number of printing errors, a work completed after his death by Bishop Richard Parry and Dr. John Davies. The revised Bible was published in 1620 and this version became the standard Welsh Bible that has remained in use to the present day. In 1595 Morgan was appointed Bishop of Llandaff, and later St. Asaph, and was much celebrated for his translation. Morgan pronounced himself unhappy with the original edition of a thousand Bibles, saying they were expensive at two pounds each and inconveniently large.

The early publications that standardised the Welsh language played a significant role in the survival of the language as they united the dialects of Wales with one formal language. We could have chosen to feature Dolbelydr, Denbighshire in this book as it was where Henry Salesbury (1561-c.1605) wrote his *Grammatica Britannica* of 1593. However, we shouldn't underestimate the significance of William Morgan's work; Wynford Vaughan-Thomas in his book *Wales – A History*, wrote that 'If ever one single book saved a language, that book is the Bible in Welsh'.

Morgan's translation gave Welsh people access to the Bible in their first, and often only, language roughly at the same time that English speakers were getting their version. The timing was crucial, as during the Tudor period the English language was being introduced in all 'formal' life in Wales, so for congregations to be able to worship in their native tongue was

significant. The Bible in Welsh and not Latin, became a document which could be accessed by all who could read, and for centuries it became the most important book in Welsh homes. Morgan's Bible was read, used regularly, and often became the place in which families inscribed their family tree and lists of births, deaths and marriages.

In 1591 George Owen of Henllys, Pembrokeshire wrote:

'We have the light of the gospel, yea, the whole Bible in our own native tongue, which in short time must needs work great good inwardly in the hearts of the people, whereas the service and sacraments in the English tongue was as strange to many or most of the simplest sort as the mass in the time of blindness was to the rest of England.'

William Morgan's Bible appeared when Welsh had declined in its official status. There was a risk that the varying dialects would diverge to a situation where communication became difficult between north and south. Morgan's work formalised the language and meant that Welsh speakers from all areas could understand one common, albeit formal, version of Welsh. With a Book of Common Prayer and Bible in Welsh being read in all parts of Wales every Sunday, the language was both preserved and standardised, becoming the strong language that we enjoy today.

Cae'r Gors

Cae'r Gors was the childhood home of author Kate Roberts, and it is now the best preserved cottage home of the upland slate quarry-workers

Cae'r Gors

People: Kate Roberts (1891-1985), novelist and publisher.

Place: A small, traditional stone cottage, probably dating from around 1800, now restored as a museum dedicated to Kate's work and her community.

Event: Cae'r Gors is symbolic not only of life in rural upland Wales but also the literary works of Kate Roberts who sustained the Welsh language and created a popular understanding of rural mountain living in early twentieth-century Wales.

Most of the buildings selected for this volume are associated with one event, industry or person. But tiny Cae'r Gors on the mountainside of Rhosgadfan in Caernarfonshire is celebrated for two reasons; it was the childhood home of author Kate Roberts, and it is now the best-preserved example of the cottage home of the upland slate quarry-workers.

It is a delight, and Wales is all the richer for Kate having presenting her tyddyn, or small holding, to the nation. Restoration by a local community trust has taken it back to how it would have been in Kate's day, and today we have a unique insight into the life of quarry-workers' homes in the early twentieth century, as well as a visual representation of the world Kate so famously depicted in her writings.

Cae'r Gors, Marsh Field, shows on the 1839 Tithe map and was probably built, like most similar cottages, somewhere in the seventy-five years that followed 1750. The ground plan of Cae'r Gors is unusual in that the single-storey cottage is two rooms deep with a 'catslide' roof to the rear. It may have started as a simple two roomed cottage, later subdivided to create more rooms as the family grew. As you look from the outside at the front you have the beudy, cowshed, to the left of the cottage, under the same local-slate roof. Across Wales we see variants of these longhouse forms where the cow is kept close to the home. We're fortunate to have Kate's original sketch of the rooms in the house with her notations to understand how each space was used. In the house itself

there are two rooms at the front, y gegin, kitchen/main room and y siamber ffrynt, parlour, with two rooms to the rear, y tŷ llaeth, dairy, and the small siamber gefn, back chamber/bedroom. She also noted that the daflod, sleeping loft, was over y siamber ffrynt. Life, as in all such cottages, revolved around the simdde fawr, the main fireplace where all cooking and heating took place and where the fire would rarely, if ever, go out. There is a second, smaller fireplace in the parlour likely to have been lit only on special occasions, or when visitors were expected. The house makes an interesting comparison with the terraced industrial-workers housing of, say, Blaenau Ffestiniog which is very different

in its feel. Here the family had a level of self-sufficiency, keeping a few animals and with a patch of land to tend.

Kate left the house when she was eighteen but the experience informed her writings for many years after. She was the daughter of a quarryman and had a unique skill in capturing daily life in Rhosgadfan. She became a significant figure in twentieth-century writing, much loved for short stories and particularly Traed Mewn Cyffion (Feet in Chains) of 1936 and Te yn y Grug of 1959 (Tea among the Heather). Today she is celebrated as Brenhines ein Llên (Queen of our Literature). Kate married Morris T. Williams in 1928 and in 1935 they moved to Denbigh and purchased the noted Welsh

publishing firm Gwasg Gee which published the Welsh language paper Y Faner; a publication which has aided the survival of Welsh in the twentieth century. Morris died in 1946 but Kate continued managing the business alone for a further ten years, publishing the newspaper and contributing to it, as well as continuing with her short stories and novels in Welsh.

By 1965 when Kate bought Cae'r Gors for the nation it had fallen into disrepair, and it took until 2005 to raise the funds to achieve the restoration and put a roof back on. In the meantime, Cadw had the cottage listed as a 'managed ruin'. The house was finally opened with an interpretation centre in 2007. The kitchen garden was restored around the cottage.

That Cae'r Gors has been taken back to pristine condition from a roofless ruin, using the skills and support of the local community and Cadw, is a reflection of how much people love Kate's work and the building itself. When you visit and sit by the fire today you wouldn't know the building had once fallen on such hard times. Instead you can feel that love. To anyone who has read Kate's work, Cae'r Gors is a place of pilgrimage, and to the nation it simply couldn't be more Welsh as a building. That one small cottage can represent so much to so many is an achievement; something that was once everyday has become iconic and irreplaceable.

"Nadolig Llawen a Blwyddyn
Newydd Dda."

"Canys ganwyd i chwi heddyw Geidwad yn ninas
Dafydd, yr hwn yw Crist yr Arglwydd."

RHAGLEN
CYFARFOD "GOBEITHLU,"
Bethel, Gaiman,
* A GYNHELIR *
NADOLIG (RHAGFYR 26), 1921.

Llywydd	- - -	Parch. JOHN FOULKES.
Arweinydd	- - -	Parch. D. D. WALTERS.
Cyfeilyddion	-	Mrs. ARTHUR ROBERTS, B.A.,
		a'r Br. EDWARD R. EVANS.

Y cyfarfod i ddechreu am 7 p.m. :: Mynediad i mewn
i Oedogion drwy Raglen, 50 sent yr un;
Plant dan 15 oed yn rhad.

COFLECH
i'r
Parchedig
JOHN CAERENIG EVANS.
(1837, — 1913.)
Bu'n weinidog yr
Eglwys hon
o'i Sylfaeniad yn
1876
hyd ei farwolaeth.

Capel Bethel, Patagonia

There are several buildings outside Wales that could lay claim to having helped build Wales and our sense of Welshness. The Palace of Westminster almost made it into the final choice as so many decisions affecting Wales have been made there. A happier 'foreigner' to include is one of the Capillas Galesas – the Welsh chapels of Patagonia, Argentina, as they represent the Welsh community that moved there in the late nineteenth and early twentieth centuries.

A hundred and fifty years ago the tall ship tea clipper Mimosa set sail from Liverpool to take a group of people from Wales to establish a new life and community in a remote valley in Patagonia. The Argentinian government had been trying to persuade people to colonise the wilderness, and granted anyone free, if marginal, land in exchange for setting up a farm. Communities moved over from Switzerland, Germany, Italy and several other countries including Wales. Most were motivated by poverty and the chance of a new life, but the first Welsh group had a different story.

The plan to establish the Welsh colony was proposed by preacher Michael

D. Jones from Bala who called for a new 'little Wales beyond Wales', parodying the expression 'Little England beyond Wales' often applied to south Pembrokeshire. For Jones, the Patagonian experiment was motivated by politics and culture; he wanted to establish a new colony in a remote area that would allow the Welsh language and non-conformist culture to thrive in ways that he felt it couldn't back at home. He was an idealist, and the people who eventually made the trip out to settle Patagonia were a mix of the like-minded as well as those motivated the chance of having their own land and a better life. Jones recruited settlers for his project, raised funds and arranged that the Argentine government would donate a hundred hectares of land for every family of settlers along the Chubut River. At the time the ownership of Patagonia wasn't clear, so it was an astute political move on behalf of the Argentine Government to give away land in exchange for loyalty to their government.

The Mimosa set off from Liverpool in May 1865, with 153 Welsh settlers aboard (56 married adults, 33 single men, 12 single women and 52 children). It had cost £2,500 to hire the ship and fit her out for

Capel Bethel, Patagonia

People: The Patagonian population; Michael D. Jones (1822-1898), minister and founder of the Wladfa colony; Elisa Evans de Williams, donor of the land in 1912; John Caerenig Evans (1837-1913), Gaiman's first minister.

Place: A classic Welsh chapel, built in brick in 1913 to a much-used pattern at Gaiman in one of the two Welsh colonies in Patagonia. In exterior form and interior detail it is identical to non-conformist chapels built in Wales.

Event: There are a number of delightful Capillas Galesas, Welsh chapels in Patagonia that could have been chosen to represent the Welsh colony there. We chose this as one of the larger chapels in a town with the most vibrant surviving Welsh culture. The colony reflects the determination of Michael D. Jones and his followers to create an idealised Welsh-speaking chapel-led culture far away from the English-speaking world and its politics.

A hundred and fifty years ago the tall-ship tea clipper Mimosa set sail from Liverpool to take a group of people from Wales to establish a new life and community in a remote valley in Patagonia

the journey. The congregation included miners, carpenters and tailors, but few agriculturalists and only one with any form of medical skill.

When they arrived in Patagonia they didn't find the Eden that had been promised, and had to cope with a harsh landscape with much less rain than they'd been led to expect. They'd left the green hills of Wales, the only landscape they'd ever seen, and arrived in a parched semi-desert landscape with little knowledge of what would grow there to feed them or how to become self-sufficient. Some died on the initial trek inland in search of fresh water and there were many early crop failures and much hardship. By 1869 the Welsh colony had reduced to just ninety as people moved to other areas of Argentina, discouraged by the irregular rainfall that either brought drought or flash flooding.

Following initial hardship the community managed to establish a good agricultural tradition by developing irrigation by around 1880, securing their colony which would expand in 1889 to the Andes in what they named 'Cwm Hyfryd'. The last group of settlers arrived from Wales in 1911, but as other nationalities moved to the area the Welsh eventually became a minority. By the turn of the twentieth century the Argentinian government was taking more notice and control of the Patagonian communities, and laws were introduced to homogenise the population into the Spanish-speaking world. There was resistance from the Welsh communities and to this day the Welsh language survives in both Welsh colonies. The National Assembly sponsors a scheme to support the Welsh language and culture in Patagonia, sending teachers over to teach the Patagonians of

Welsh descent.

The small town of Gaiman on the banks of the Chubut River is the place where you get the strongest sense of Welsh culture if visiting today. The Municipal Council was formed in 1885 after a group of houses started to take shape in 1875 following the construction of the first 'Tŷ Cerrig' which was later used as the Gaiman branch of the Cwmni Masnachol Camwy. The name Gaiman means 'rocky point' in the native Tehuelche language and historically the Welsh settlers had a much better relationship with the indigenous population than many other colonising groups. Today around 6,000 people live in Gaiman and there is a popular Eisteddfod every October. The hub of the community is Capel Bethel.

The Welsh settlers built Welsh cottages and Welsh chapels according to the only

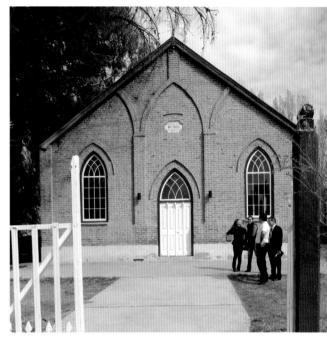

architectural tradition they knew, and Capel Bethel is a classic non-conformist chapel. To look at the building you wouldn't know you weren't in Wales, apart from perhaps the trees around that probably wouldn't feel at home in Wales. The brickwork, the Gothic arched windows, the proportion of the whole is entirely Welsh, as indeed were many of the buildings the early Welsh built in Patagonia. Inside is a perfect Welsh chapel interior with Gothic revival pitch-pine pews and Welsh language memorial plaques on the wall. The chapel is a classic non-conformist Anibynnol, Independent chapel built as late as 1913. The names of those associated with its construction will tell you how strong the Welsh culture was in Gaiman. Bethel was built on land donated by Elisa Evans de Williams. The first minister was John Caerenig Evans, and the builders were

Jack Jones, Llewelyn Griffiths and Egryn Evans. Today you'll still find names that represent the cultural mix and we're grateful to Fernando Williams for the photographs here.

The Welsh chapels of the Chubut valley have been essential in maintaining the culture and language of the Welsh community in Patagonia. The Welsh language still survives but is now more of a cultural symbol to most than their everyday tongue. The economy of Gaiman thrives on its Welshness, with a number of Welsh tearooms that are packed at weekends when the wealthy head into this tiny interior town to enjoy the heritage and book a table laden with cakes and sandwiches. To the Argentinians, Welsh culture means 'high tea' culture, and they'll come, visit the museum and chapel, perhaps take a tour down the valley to see further chapels,

and then head back to Gaiman for an immense feast of cream cakes.

You won't hear much Welsh spoken in the three main settlements of Gaiman, Trelew or Trevelin, but you will see the language in signage, in the names of streets, farms, shops and tearooms. And if you ask you won't have to look far to find people who can speak the language. Considering the waves of incomers into Welsh-speaking Patagonia it is remarkable that the language has survived at all, but it has because of the proud patriotism of the Welsh inhabitants there. That community was one built on chapel culture, and it is only right that they remain proud of their Welsh heritage.

Neuadd Pantycelyn

'the residential expression of the University's commitment to the language, culture and people of Wales'

Is Pantycelyn a concept that could exist outside of the current building? Or has the building become synonymous with the protection of the Welsh language? In 2014, Pantycelyn celebrated its fortieth birthday, having been home to several thousand Welsh speakers during their time at Aberystwyth University. It has formed a close-knit community of students and has a glitterati of alumni. In 2015, at the time of writing, there is a storm brewing over the future of this famous hall of residence. Students are protesting on the roof against possible closure, but Aberystwyth University is adamant it will reopen after a several million pound refurbishment. In 2008 the building was listed Grade II in an effort to safeguard its historic exteriors. Pantycelyn is described by Aberystwyth University as being 'the residential expression of the University's commitment to the language, culture and people of Wales'.

Percy Thomas designed the halls of residence in a robust, low neo-Georgian style, reminiscent of the American universities of the period. A far grander affair had been originally envisaged, with a square central pavilion. The grey ashlar walls, with large framed rectangular windows, strike comparison with Thomas' contemporary Carmarthen County Hall (1938-58). Percy Thomas was born in South Shields but spent most of his working life in Wales, and his Cardiff-based practice still bears his name.

The halls opened in 1951 just below the main University Campus, sharing its site with the National Library of Wales. Pantycelyn is named after William Williams (1717-1791), the bard and hymn-writer whose famous words 'Guide me, O Thou great Jehovah' still resonate so strongly through the Welsh psyche. Born in Carmarthenshire, Williams was an aspiring cleric in the Anglican Church. After a refusal by the local bishop in 1743 to ordain Williams as a priest, he turned his attention to the Methodist movement, becoming one of its leaders in Wales. He travelled the length and breadth of the country with religious zeal, converting, preaching and producing a large corpus of Methodist hymns in both English and Welsh. He was ardently bi-lingual, translating vast tracts into Welsh from English and vice versa. He realised the power of language, and sought to protect it. Poetry was another form of expression for which Williams became well known, about which he exercised considerable influence over his contemporaries.

With such associations, it is no wonder that the concept of Pantycelyn Halls holds such a passionate view for many Welsh speakers. Alumni liken it to the freshman dormitories of American universities such as Harvard. The sense of community, cohesion and comradery is strong, and for undergraduates it provides a safe environment for those who have just left home. The late Dr. John Davies was appointed Warden of Pantycelyn when it first opened as a Welsh-only hall, continuing in this role for 18 years until 1992. Five years before Davies took over, the Prince of Wales took up residence in room ninety-five of Pantycelyn whilst he was studying Welsh at Aberystwyth during the summer of 1969. The royal entourage occupied a section of the upper floor at Pantycelyn, in part of the building now nicknamed 'the royal suite.'

Whatever the future holds for Pantycelyn, it has had an illustrious history. The building will surely always remain, but whether it will continue to be the home of Welsh-speaking 'Aber' undergraduates is in the hands of the University.

Neuadd Pantycelyn

People: Designed by Sir Percy Thomas (1883-1969) in 1939, but not executed as a Hall of Residence until after World War II in 1951.

Place: An evocative and palimpsest building that symbolises the movement to protect Welsh language and culture.

Event: Since 1973, Pantycelyn has been the scene of many protests and demonstrations against perceived threats to the Welsh language.

Bangor
University

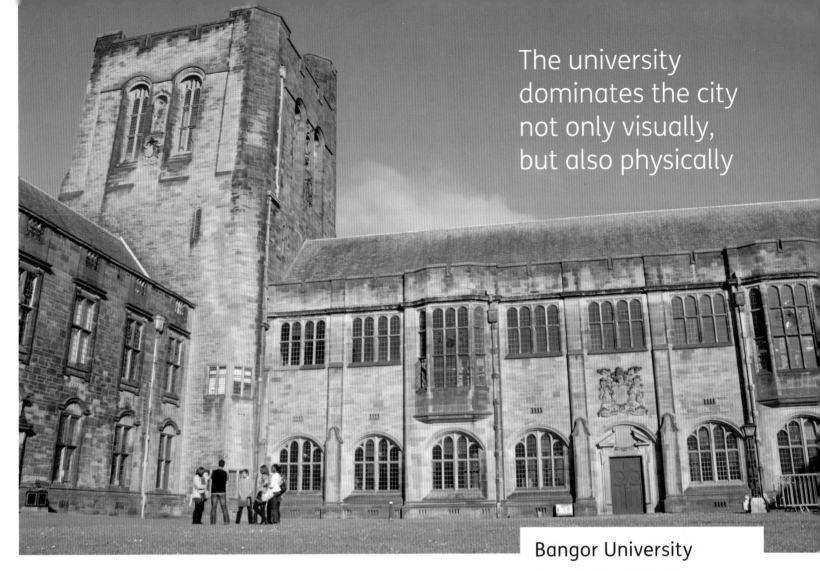

The university dominates the city not only visually, but also physically

Bangor University

People: The Main Arts building was designed by Henry Thomas Hare (1861-1921) and was completed in 1911.

Place: There was a great desire to provide higher education in Wales, and in 1884 the University College of North Wales was founded. Bangor was in competition with some of the other towns in north Wales for the founding of its first university.

Event: During World War Two, many works of art from the great galleries of Central London were given safe haven within the great Pritchard Jones Hall.

Bangor's location, between the edge of Snowdonia and the Menai Strait, is the most dramatic setting of any university in Wales, and is scarcely matched by the rest of the UK. The university dominates the city not only visually, but also physically. Being a student at Bangor is like being in a bubble. It's far enough from other big centres of population to have enough space to develop its own character, yet close enough to escape for a day in Dublin, Chester, Liverpool or Manchester. This is one of the main attractions of Bangor to students; while it's secluded it's not divorced from the rest of the world. For many English students, Bangor is exotic. Stunningly beautiful in the sun, dark and mysterious in the wet, it is often the first taste of Wales for many, with many becoming seduced by the alluring charms of the locals or the drama of the surrounding scenery.

Founded in 1884 as University College of North Wales, it received its Royal Charter a year later. There had been a thirst to improve education in north Wales and competition was strong amongst the towns as to which would house its maiden

university. Bangor was chosen and the new university was based in an old coaching inn, the Penrhyn Arms, situated on the road into the city by Penrhyn Castle.

Henry Thomas Hare's imposing new University College, now the Main Arts building, was built in a robust Jacobean style, soaring above Bangor as a successor to the medieval cathedral. Hare intended it to be a homage to the monastic origins of city. The buildings were constructed around quadrangles, with the Prichard-Jones Hall (nicknamed PJ Hall) as the centrepiece. Sir Richard

Prichard-Jones (1841-1917) was a wealthy, self-made businessman from Anglesey who rose through the ranks of the Regent Street based department store, Dickins and Jones, to become a partner. He was to be one of Bangor's greatest benefactors. During World War Two, PJ Hall housed some of Britain's most important works of art to protect them from German bombing raids. After bombing Liverpool, German aircraft lightened their loads before making the trip back so many coastal towns along the north Wales coast were inadvertently bombed. As this threat increased, the

works of art were transferred from Bangor to the underground slate caverns in Blaenau Ffestiniog.

Famous students of Bangor are numerous, but include Welsh writer Kate Roberts (1891-1985); director and producer, Danny Boyle; and poet, R. S. Thomas (1913-2000).

Pentre Ifan

The site sits against a horizon dominated by Carningli mountain which may have been spiritually significant in ancient times

The megalithic dolmen of Pentre Ifan that stands near Nevern in Pembrokeshire was probably never built to house anyone, and yet is most definitely a structure that has helped to create people's sense of Wales. We assume the monument was constructed in the Bronze Age (2300 – 800 BC), though some suggest Neolithic (4000-2500 BC). Since the seventeenth century it has become associated with ideas about Celts, druids and the indigenous Welsh. It is a good example of how we apply cultural associations to built structures, whether or not they are actually drawn from the evidence at hand.

Seven large stones form the version of Pentre Ifan that we see today, with a group of three orthostats holding what appears to be an unfeasibly large capstone some 5 metres long, two and a half metres wide, orientated north-south and possibly weighing sixteen tonnes. Nobody knows for sure why the dolmen was constructed, but the general consensus is that it formed the inner chamber of a large rock and soil covered mound and that it was used for communal burial, similar to Bryn Celli Ddu in Anglesey. The assumption is that the site has been dramatically excavated by treasure hunters looking for gold, and that all remains is this inner core structure.

No burial remains have been found during the two excavations of 1936-7 and 1958-9, and indeed there is no real evidence of where the substantial amount of removed waste has gone. A recent theory by Cummings & Richard (2014) proposes that the site was built in its existing state as a landmark and/or

Pentre Ifan

People: The Bronze age communities of south-west Wales 2300-800 BC, George Owen of Henllys (1552-1613), antiquarian; William Stukeley (1687-1765), clergyman and antiquarian.

Place: An unusually large dolmen, interpreted as having started life as a Bronze Age burial chamber on the slopes of Carn Ingli mountain near Nevern in Pembrokeshire.

Event: Even though the archaeological evidence is not clear, and there is much misunderstanding and misuse of the term Celtic, monuments such as Pentre Ifan have become part of what many imagine was ancient Celtic Welsh life. and represent ancient Wales.

demonstration of engineering prowess. The site sits against a horizon dominated by Carningli Mountain which may have been spiritually significant in ancient times. The archaeologist George Nash has suggested the structure may even be a miniature representation or homage to the mountain behind. At the end of the day it is an archaeological monument, and we'll probably never be quite sure of its intended purpose.

Whether the dolmen was built as a standing monument or as the inner core of a burial chamber is irrelevant. Romantic ideas have been associated with the site since the seventeenth century. Antiquarian George Owen wrote about the place as early as 1603, and since then it has become part of the

Bryn Celli Ddu

tourist trail for those interested in ancient history. William Stukeley, who pioneered the archaeological investigations at Stonehenge and Avebury, took an interest in the site. He was famously ordained a druid and a leading figure in neo-druidry, and commissioned a now iconic engraving of the dolmen which exaggerates the proportions and appears to show a man on horseback under the capstone (which in reality stands 2.5m off the ground). Pentre Ifan became a kind of Stonehenge for Wales and associated with concepts of ancient druids and Celts in popular imagination.

People associate the terms druid and Celt with Wales and Pentre Ifan and, for many, the dolmen is a perfect example of the archaeological culture that interests

them. Whether Wales is indeed Celtic is a complex debate, and the term itself is certainly problematic. Those who choose to believe in Celtic spiritualism tend not to worry that their idealised image of prehistory in Wales actually blends cultural groups from over several millennia. Debates about authenticity aside, it remains that many people want to believe that Wales is essentially Celtic, and sites like Pentre Ifan have become a place of pilgrimage as a result. The nearby Iron Age hill-fort reconstruction of Castell Henllys provides further fuel to their interest.

It isn't the case that the Romans and Anglo-Saxons invaded and populated England, and that the Welsh population retained something which was pure,

pre-Roman and therefore Celtic. However, DNA analysis such as the recent DNA Cymru project does show that there is a remarkable amount of pre-Roman blood remaining in the Welsh population. Yet even without the science, many in Wales feel that there exists a fundamental difference between themselves and their English neighbours in terms of heritage and history. Sites like Pentre Ifan have become points where the Welsh can lock onto ideas of the ancient and, being archaeology, apply what may be modern ideas to the ancient stones. Yet we shouldn't criticise this out of hand, as all history contains an element of selection, a reading of events and timescales through a process which is without question fraught with bias. We make and define

the history we want, as individuals, as communities and as a nation, and Pentre Ifan provides an appropriate site on which to project ideas of what we think ancient Wales once was.

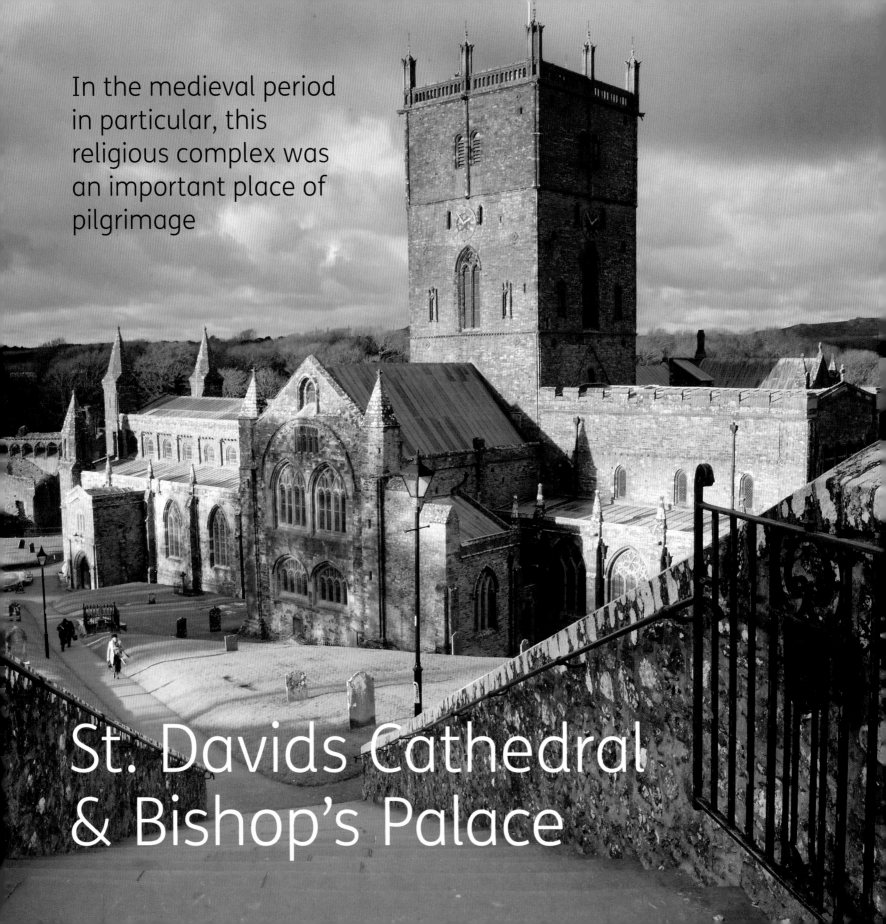

In the medieval period in particular, this religious complex was an important place of pilgrimage

St. Davids Cathedral & Bishop's Palace

St. Davids Cathedral

People: St David (c500-589), Bishop and later Patron Saint of Wales; William I (C1028-1087), known as William the Conqueror; Pope Calixtus II (c1065-1124); Bishop Peter de Leia (died 1198), built the 'Romanesque' Cathedral we see today; Henry II (1133-1189); Edward I (1239-1307); Oliver Cromwell (1599-1658); John Nash (1752-1835), architect; Sir George Gilbert Scott (1811-1878), architect.

Place: A much-altered though essentially Romanesque period cathedral dedicated to St David, with associated important early buildings in the small Pembrokeshire city which takes its name.

Event: Of immense significance and influence in the medieval world of Britain, and it remains the main Welsh Cathedral to this day. Significant now as the place most associated with the Patron Saint of Wales.

There are several wonderful cathedrals in Wales and none of them insignificant. However, the cathedral at St. Davids has played a special role in the development of our country. In the medieval period in particular, this religious complex was an important place of pilgrimage, and the tiny city beside it held a status far above its meagre size. St. Davids was a powerhouse of Welsh ecclesiastical and intellectual culture, and celebrated throughout Britain.

St David established the strict monastic community at the site named after him

The significance of the site is reflected in visits from William the Conqueror in 1077, Henry II in 1171, and Edward I in 1284

before his death in 589. He was the most influential clergyman in all Wales during the so called 'Age of Saints'. Today a reliquary behind the High Altar is said to hold his bones as well as those of St. Justinian, his colleague and confessor. The early monastic community was often attacked by Vikings among others, and several bishops were murdered including Bishop Moregenau in 999 and Bishop Abraham in 1080. The original cathedral built on the site was often plundered and was finally burnt and destroyed in 1087. In 1123, Pope Calixtus II decreed that two pilgrimages to St. Davids were equivalent to one to Rome ('Roma semel quantum dat bis Menevia tantum'), a decree which gave a substantial boost to the status of the cathedral as well as to the economy of the town, as a vast income was raised from visiting pilgrims in the Middle Ages.

The significance of the site is reflected in visits from William the Conqueror in 1077, Henry II in 1171, and Edward I in 1284. Before reliable roads, the pilgrims arrived by boat, at Porth Clais, where St

David was baptised. There are shrines and chapels dotted along the Welsh coast where they would have rested on their journey and given thanks for safe passage. The area remains rich in early Christian heritage to this day. St. Davids occupied a strategic position in medieval times at the junction of major land and sea routes between England, Wales and Ireland. It is said that St Patrick (himself Welsh) set sail from here on his mission to convert Ireland to Christianity. Britain's smallest city, no larger than a village today, has always punched above its weight.

The building you see today, like most early cathedrals, has a complex history. It takes a detailed analysis to understand the various builds which have been complicated by several restorations. In principle the cathedral dates from the twelfth to sixteenth centuries, with restorations and rebuilding by John Nash (1793) and Sir George Gilbert Scott (1862-78). Despite these restorations the character of the building is substantially the cathedral as built by Bishop Peter de Leia in the 'Romanesque' style. This makes it a delight among British cathedrals, being essentially complete before the Gothic style took over. The west front is a restoration by Gilbert Scott to recreate the Norman original following a structurally unsuccessful restoration by John Nash in 1793. In 1220 the central tower fell, demolishing the choir and transepts, but they were rebuilt to a very similar design by 1250. There have been various other collapses (one from an earthquake) and significant destruction by Oliver Cromwell's forces in

the seventeenth century. The carved oak misericords in the late fifteenth-century choir are a particular delight as are some important early Tudor, and other tombs and effigies.

St. Davids is the principal cathedral of Wales and one of the most important medieval ecclesiastical buildings in Britain. The fourteenth-century former Bishop's Palace (derelict since the eighteenth century) that stands next door is similarly significant. The building still inspires awe in visitors today, more than eight hundred years after it was constructed. Imagine then, the reaction of the medieval visitor, travelling across the Pembrokeshire landscape of humble thatch and slated cottages, to come across such a wonderful building. Most visitors today make a pilgrimage to St. Davids as part of a family holiday rather than through religious duty.

Capel Soar-y-Mynydd

Capel Soar-y-Mynydd

People: The congregation of Capel Soar-y-Mynydd (constructed 1822); Rev. Ebenezer Richard (1781-1837), Calvinistic Methodist minister; John Jones of Nant Llwyd Farm; Ogwyn Davies (1925-1915); Harri Webb (1920-1994), Anglo-Welsh poet; Iwan Llwyd (1957-2010), poet.

Place: Early 1820 stone-built non-conformist Welsh upland chapel in a particularly remote location in the hills above Llanddewi Brefi, Ceredigion.

Event: Often described as the most remote chapel in Wales. The fight to keep it open and in use brought together people from all religious groups in Wales and today the place is seen as iconic of rural chapel culture and architecture.

It has been noted that, on average, one chapel closes in Wales every week. When this happens another piece of Welsh community and heritage is lost. This couldn't be a book on Welsh architecture without the inclusion of at least one non-conformist chapel as, by the start of the twentieth century, Wales had broken free from the Anglican tradition to become an essentially non-conformist country. Non-conformist was a term used in England and Wales after the Act of Uniformity of 1662 to refer to a Protestant Christian who did not 'conform' to the governance of the established Church of England. For the last two centuries non-conformist chapels of various denominations have been central buildings in Welsh daily life; built by local subscription, lovingly tended, often expanded and rebuilt: the pride of their communities.

Non-conformity had a significant influence on the cultural, political and social life of Wales, as well as its religion. For such a small country Wales has an impressive number of chapels: over 6,000 which, in their heyday, were often rebuilt and expanded to accommodate increasing local demand. The four main denominations were the Calvinistic Methodists, Congregationalists (also known as the Independents), Baptists and Wesleyans, though there was a significant flourishing of Unitarians in the Teifi valley as well as Quaker groups in various places. Most people in Wales would have attended a chapel at least once a week, making the buildings central in their community. During the 1904-1905 Digwyddiad, Revival, an estimated extra 100,000 people flocked to local chapels, and there were scenes of virtual hysteria in some Ceredigion chapels as the new

members came to hear the famous speakers of the day.

Wales has been left with a rich architectural heritage of chapels built by non-conformist protestant communities that didn't want to follow the Gothic revival styles popular in the Anglican Church. You can stand outside a non-conformist chapel and know it is exactly that before you learn which denomination it was built for. The simple forms, arrangement of windows (often related to the location of the pulpit on a long side wall) and two-storey height to accommodate an interior upper balcony all say non-conformist. Decoration tends to be restrained and elegant rather than free-flowing and fanciful. These chapels were built at much lower cost than the elaborate edifices of the Anglican and Catholic churches and were deliberately 'simple prayer rooms' reflecting Puritan worshipping practices espoused by Calvin and others. The plainest among them are almost industrial in appearance, with others appearing domestic in their form and styling.

Religious fervour for non-conformism has waned, and it can be difficult to find new uses for these large buildings that don't ruin their internal proportions. Unfortunately the most popular new use

'God is love'

for them, residential conversion, is one of the least suitable for a building that it is essentially one large space with a ceiling so high that it is difficult to heat. When people 'carve them up' into smaller boxes

the sense of the original is lost, and a piece of Welsh history with it.

Capel Soar-y-Mynydd perched high on the far eastern extremity of the community of Llanddewi Brefi in Ceredigion is known as capel mwyaf pellennig/anghysbell Cymru gyfan – Wales' remotest chapel. The building is handsome if not exceptional, built with chapel and chapel house for the caretaker, all under one long roof, almost as a larger version of the longhouses that are common in this remote upland area.

Soar was constructed in 1822, only a year after the Calvinistic Methodists established their independence. It was the idea of Rev. Ebenezer Richard of Tregaron to provide a chapel serving the dispersed rural communities of upland Ceredigion and land was provided by John Jones, farmer at Nant-Llwyd. The chapel is a simple yet charming structure built from the local rubble stone collected from ruined farmsteads and the local riverbed, then limewashed. The pulpit, as in many early non-conformist chapels, is placed between the two doorways on the side elevation, as if making a point about 'high Church' Anglicanism where the congregation were preached to from high pulpits that separated the minister from the congregation. Above the pulpit is a painted scroll and the maxim 'Duw cariad yw' (God is love). Next door stands the simple chapel house, also Listed, where the local school ran until the 1940s.

The biblical Zoar, after which Soar takes its name, was spared by God when the cities of Sodom and Gomorrah were destroyed (Genesis 19:20-30), and our Mountain Zoar (Soar-y-Mynydd) has

also been spared the fate of many of its sister chapels: closure and dereliction or insensitive conversion. As early as 1968 the congregation had fallen to just two individuals as the rural upland depopulated, and it seemed that closure was inevitable. Yet, almost as if the hand of God was involved, Wales' remotest chapel has been spared and today is one of the most loved and celebrated chapels in all of Wales.

Soar was formally reopened in 1973 and there was a campaign to keep the building in use. Today people travel from across Wales to attend the sporadic services there, and the summer service on the last Sunday in August has become an annual pilgrimage for many. The services continue in the Welsh language as they always have been. Soar has become iconic within Welsh-speaking Wales, and has been photographed and painted many times, notably by Ogwyn Davies in 1993 who created a very popular print of the chapel formed from the lines of the hymns of non-conformism. It also features in the poetry of Harri Webb and Iwan Llwyd, among others.

Wales is a small country with a deeply rooted heritage and a strong connection to its cultural and religious roots. It seemed inevitable that the remotest chapel in Wales must close if there wasn't a local congregation to support it, but the Welsh people (and particularly Welsh speakers) have saved this handsome chapel as a cultural icon. The people who make pilgrimages to Soar-y-Mynydd aren't all Calvinistic Methodists. Many probably don't even regularly attend any religious service. However, they all

The summer service on the last Sunday in August has become an annual pilgrimage for many

love Wales and this building has become symbolic, both to them and to others, of a great deal of what Wales means. If the most inaccessible chapel in Wales that has no feasible local congregation can be saved, then surely we can act to save more of the built heritage that represents our country?

Capel y Tabernacl

Capel y Tabernacl

People: The chapel was designed by the architect John Humphrey and built at a cost of £15,000 in 1872.

Place: This is one of the largest non-conformist chapels in Wales, holding a congregation of around 3000. It was given the moniker 'The Cathedral of Wales'.

Event: For certain sections of Welsh society, the chapel dominated their everyday lives. The power of the minister permeated every layer of life, for both good and bad.

Capel y Tabernacl represents the peak of chapel construction and its dominance in the everyday life of people in Wales. Religious architecture was a community engagement and nearly 7,000 chapels were constructed across the country. They have become, through sheer volume, an important physical reminder of a cultural and social period in Welsh history, one which spans the centuries but which reached its highest level towards the end of the nineteenth century. The industrialisation of south Wales brought rapid increases in population, in line with the boom and bust heavy industries. In the Swansea Valley, mass migration took place, with rural workers moving to areas where work was plentiful. As a result, nonconformity found easy expression within these new communities.

Capel y Tabernacl could be said to the largest and most expensive chapel to have been built in Wales. Nicknamed the 'Non-conformist Cathedral of Wales', work on the ambitious structure was completed in 1872 at a cost of £15,000 – a huge amount of money but representative of the amassed wealth from the coal, steel, copper and tin industries of the Swansea region. It was designed by architect John Humphrey with much input from

the chapel minister, Emlyn Jones, and contractor, Daniel Edwards. The original chapel had proven to be too small for a growing congregation of 800 and a new building was needed. When completed, the new chapel had seating for 3,000 and, although membership never reached this size, in 1910, following the 1904 Revival, numbers peaked at over 1,000.

It was listed Grade I for being the most ambitious chapel in Wales, noted by

Cadw, for its 'striking exterior presence, and virtually unaltered interior and fittings'. John Humphrey's original drawings survive, and the side elevations are reminiscent of Alfred Waterhouse's idiosyncratic Romanesque style. The overall building is eclectic, Gothic in part, classical in another. The main front is temple-like, with four pairs of unfluted Corinthian columns, of the giant order. To its side is a 160-foot Gothic tower, with spire on top. Internally, the amphitheatre

quality is breath-taking, focussing on the large convex pulpit. Today, membership stands at just below 150 and the choir, formed in 1876, is one of the oldest mixed Welsh choirs still performing.

Chapel culture was central to the life of many: prayer meetings, bible study, coffee mornings, Sunday schools, male voice choirs, brass and silver bands and military bands, were all features of the chapel community. The remnants of this this are still around today, but greatly

Chapel culture was central to the life of many: prayer meetings, bible study, coffee mornings, Sunday schools, male voice choirs, brass and silver bands and military bands, were all features of the chapel community

diminished in terms of participation, if not enthusiasm. Wales is recognised for its surviving medieval military architecture, rural farmhouses, vernacular cottages and nineteenth-century chapels, but the latter are slowly dying out, often being converted for commercial and residential dwellings. The Royal Commission, working with the Chapels Heritage Society, have been recording the several thousand chapels that were built in Wales so that even if their physical presence may no longer be viable, their traditions and significance will be retained for future generations.

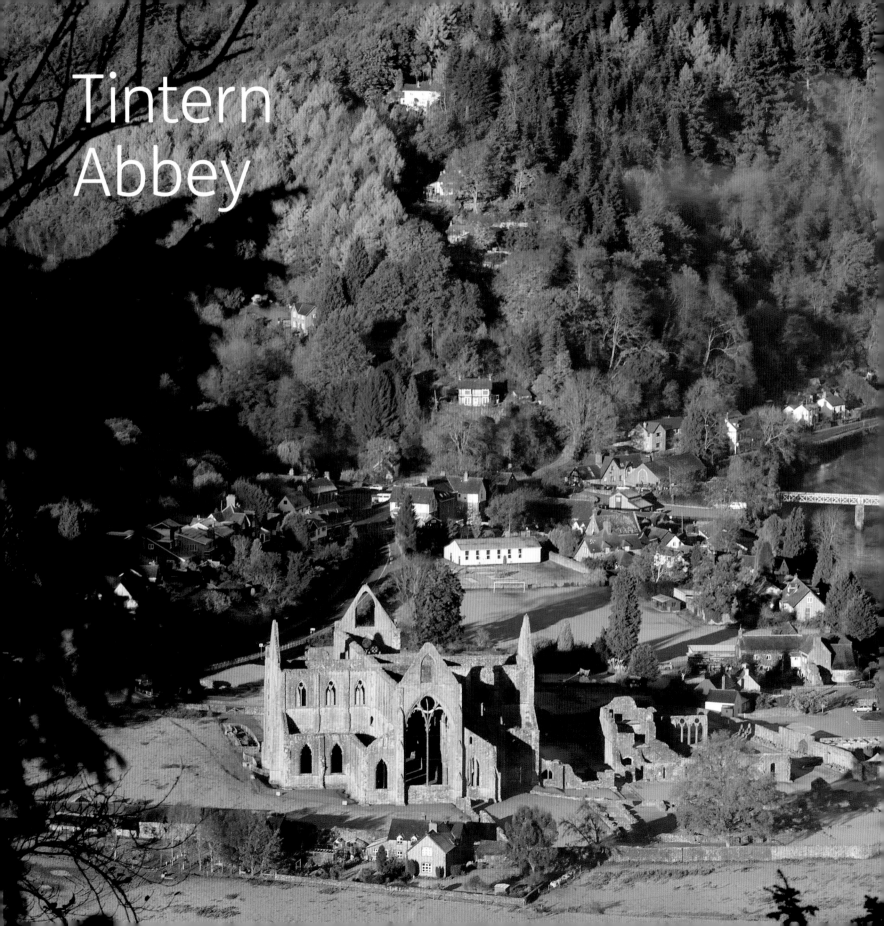

Tintern Abbey

The monks, who came from the abbey of l'Aumône in France, were granted land in a suitably remote location, as befitting the requirements of the Cistercians

Tintern Abbey

People: The abbey was founded by Walter de Clare, Lord of Chepstow (died 1137/1138) in 1131.

Place: Monastic life was a dominant force in Wales until the Dissolution of the Monasteries during the 1530s.

Event: It was the first Cistercian monastery to be founded in Wales and the second in Britain.

Tintern Abbey was the first Cistercian abbey to be founded in Wales. The monastic orders shaped medieval society profoundly, mainly by having large landholdings and accumulating great wealth and power. Tintern was founded in 1131 by the variously named Walter fitz Richard de Clare, Lord of Chepstow. The monks, who came from the abbey of l'Aumône in France, were granted land in a suitably remote location, as befitting the requirements of the Cistercians. Religious life was regimented and followed strict rules. Whether these rules were adhered to is open to debate, as many accounts of abuses have survived in the historical record.

During the first half of the thirteenth century the abbey buildings were expanded around a magnificent Gothic church which was dedicated to the Virgin Mary. To the north was the cloister, in which the monks exercised or worked at desks due to the good lighting from the many windows. The monks would have listened to readings of the Bible in the evenings, which were read aloud by

the abbot. The functional heart of the abbey was the chapter house where all business was transacted and conversation permitted. Food was served in the refectory, or dining hall, where again religious readings were read aloud during meal times. Either side of the refectory were the kitchens and warming house. The latter of these was the only heated room, where a fire was kept from All Souls' Day (November 1) until Good Friday.

Four hundred years after its foundation, in September 1535, Tintern surrendered to Henry VIII's Dissolution of the Monasteries. All buildings, land and wealth were taken by the crown, and the land redistributed. Tintern was given to Henry Somerset, Earl of Worcester, who set about developing the former religious lands. Industry was fostered in the Wye Valley, where iron wire was produced and communities began to flourish. The abbey was quarried for building materials and the church became a picturesque ruin. Antiquarians rediscovered Tintern in the eighteenth century as the Romantic Movement took hold. Tourists began flocking to view the 'sublime' ruins, evoking a distant past with an air of divine decay. Travellers would come by boat from Ross-on-Wye to visit the remains which gained greater prominence by being painted by J. M. W. Turner around 1794, and forming the subject of poetical works by William Wordsworth (1798) and Alfred, Lord Tennyson (1847). The evocative site inspired many an artist and traveller, putting Wales on the map as a popular destination for tourists across Europe.

Tintern is not only a part of Wales' medieval religious heritage, but also an important visitor attraction, helping to build this key facet of the Welsh economy. Reverend William Gilpin's *Observations on the River Wye* were published in 1782

The evocative site inspired many an artist and traveller, putting Wales as a destination for tourists across Europe

and the picturesque movement's adherents arrived in droves to see the ivy-clad remains. By means of protection, the abbey site was purchased in 1901 by the Crown who carried out major repair works which lasted nearly thirty years. In 1984, Tintern passed into the care of Cadw, who opened the site to the public. One little known fact is that Iron Maiden filmed their 1988 music video *Can I Play with Madness* at Tintern. Would the monks have approved?

St David's College

Having the first Royal Charter granted for a university in England or Wales outside Oxford or Cambridge makes St David's College, Lampeter, a building that built Wales. This college brought university education to the nation in 1822. Lampeter holds a special place within the hearts of the Welsh; a tiny Welsh-speaking rural market town of the Teifi valley which has punched above its weight in academia and culture since a college was first established there two centuries ago. The university remains one of the most charming campuses in Britain, and has long attracted academics of a calibre above its small size.

The idea to establish university-level education at Lampeter goes back to Thomas Burgess, appointed Bishop of St David's in 1803. Burgess recognised that Welsh ordinands were effectively denied higher level education by the distance and cost incurred in travel to Oxford. He wanted to build in nearby Llanddewi Brefi, but landowner John Scandrett Harford donated a three acre site around the remains of the Norman castle in Lampeter. Harford himself built an attractive Italianate villa at nearby Falcondale, now a hotel. The new college structure was built immediately adjacent to, and partially on, the Norman motte in a restrained Tudor style.

The college was founded in 1822 and completed by 1827, opening on St David's day and welcoming its first twenty-six students. The £16,000 project was funded by donations from the public and from King George IV, who granted the first charter in 1828. C. R. Cockerell was chosen as the architect and a reduced version of his originally very grand plan was constructed, loosely based on an Oxford medieval college around a quadrangle, with lecture rooms, student accommodation, a dining hall, chapel and library all within the core building. The Old Hall was the rectory until 1969 when it was retired. It has since become the principal space for public receptions.

The building itself was clearly built to a budget with simple Tudor arches, a crenellated parapet on the central tower, and perhaps too much simple stucco

render. Although from a distance the buildings have an elegance, close up there's a feeling that the budget ran out before completion. The chapel is the chief delight, consecrated in 1827 but remodelled in 1879 by architect Thomas Graham Jackson of Cambridge, and with a handsome 1930s oak reredos. The old library and dining hall provide other interest.

Lampeter continued as a centre of training for the clergy until 1978, but was awarding Bachelor of Arts degrees from 1865, long before the other Welsh universities. It continues as a Liberal Arts institution to this day, teaching only Humanities subjects and with strength in the Theology and Archaeology departments. After two centuries the place remains human in scale, with around a thousand students.

The town has thrived from its relationship with the university and has a multicultural buzz that would otherwise be rare in rural Wales. These days St David's College has been subsumed into the awkwardly named University of Wales Trinity Saint David (merged with Trinity College, Carmarthen), as economies of scale meant that it wasn't viable as an independent institution. When you visit today some of the energy seems to have been drawn out of the place by recent changes, which is a great shame, but it won't be long before the place is alive again. For Lampeter, the University is a life-blood, and for Wales it is a cultural and educational centre that will long enhance our country.

St David's College

People: Thomas Burgess (1756-1837), Bishop of St. Davids; George IV (1762-1830), granted the royal charter; John Scandrett Harford (1785-1866), landowner; Charles Robert Cockerell (1788-1863), architect; Thomas Graham Jackson (1835-1924), architect of the chapel.

Place: Early 1820s 'Oxford'-style University college designed by C. R. Cockerell around a quadrangle in the small Teifi valley Ceredigion town of Llanbedr Pont Steffan (Lampeter).

Event: Of British significance as the earliest University in England and Wales after Oxford and Cambridge, and important to Wales as it meant that clergy could be educated without the long and expensive travel to Oxford. An academic centre of excellence in the late twentieth century.

The Senedd

The night of 18th September 1997 was a nerve-racking one in Wales, and anyone interested in the future of our country got very little sleep. It was the counting of the results for the devolution vote to see if the people of Wales wanted to achieve a degree of independence from Westminster. This was the second referendum held in Wales over the question of devolution, the first having being heavily defeated back in 1979. Unlike the referendum in Scotland just a week earlier, there was no proposal for the Welsh assembly to have tax-varying powers and the 'No' campaign pushed a message that Wales was voting for a 'talking shop'.

The results finally settled at a sweat-inducing 50.3% Yes to 49.7% No, with the larger populations in the counties bordering England swelling the No vote: Monmouthshire voted 67.9% against, Newport 62.5%. Interestingly even Cardiff voted No (55.6%), perhaps oblivious to the wealth that the decision would bring. In fact the results map, with the exception of Pembrokeshire, showed a clear East-West divide for Yes (West) and No (East), reflecting the relative Anglicisation of Welsh geography. That vote set in motion a significant change in the governance of Wales, and our most obvious choice for a building that built Wales is the Senedd in Cardiff Bay.

At first people expected that Cardiff City Hall would become home to the Assembly, though the Coal Exchange, the former Glamorgan County Hall and

The Senedd

People: Richard Rogers (born 1933), architect; Ron Davies (born 1946), politician.

Place: A contemporary glass, slate and wood debating chamber built for the Welsh government 2001-2006, sitting on the waterside in Cardiff Bay.

Event: The first new government building for Wales in centuries reflects the optimism and changes in Welsh political culture at the turn of the millennium.

even Swansea's marvellous Guildhall were also considered. There was disagreement between the leader of Cardiff Council, Russell Goodway, and the Secretary of State for Wales, Ron Davies, over the value of the building and the cost of rehousing the council staff. Ron Davies offered the market price of £3.5m, the valuation being provided by the District Valuer. Goodway pointedly ignored valuations and insisted on £14m. In the end the deal fell through, although it is perhaps worth noting that the new building ended up costing five times that at almost £70m. It is perhaps appropriate that a political house had such a political birth.

The design for the new Senedd fell to an international architecture competition, with Davies asking for a building 'to capture the imagination of the Welsh people' and to cost no more than £12m including fees. Richard Rogers Partnership won the contract, though, as noted above, the actual cost ended up being almost six times the maximum stipulated. A fine

piece of architecture has been created, but it remains to be seen if it has indeed 'captured the imagination' of the nation, as the building has been slightly upstaged by the impressive Wales Millennium Centre built next door at approximately the same time. For the first time in centuries the Welsh people had a direct say in the decisions that affected their lives, and it is appropriate that Rogers designed a 'transparent' building that invites the public in to see how those decisions are made.

The Senedd is essentially a debating chamber with committee rooms added. The structure is remarkably simple; in fact it doesn't at first appear as a building, more an immense cover to a debating chamber with glazed-in sides, a little like the covers you see for delicate archaeology in the Mediterranean. Rogers suggested he wanted the building to feel open, not closed:

'Rather it would be a transparent envelope, looking outwards to Cardiff Bay and beyond, making visible the inner workings

of the Assembly and encouraging public participation in the democratic process.'

He certainly achieved this, but so much glass has been used in creating this transparent effect that the building appears to lack substance and from the outside, at least, reminds one of an immense greenhouse. The main elevation onto the water is dominated by giant stairs which perhaps contradict the message of accessibility a little. Inside is more successful, where three floors centre around a round debating chamber with a huge, yet elegant, wooden funnel being the main feature. It was perhaps an unfortunate choice for a debating chamber as it reminds one of a giant extractor fan, perhaps sucking the hot air created within. These criticisms aside, you only have to look to the architectural mess created for the Scottish Parliament to give thanks to Rogers for such a simple and attractive piece of architecture. The woodwork of the roof and funnel are particularly beautifully crafted.

A thousand tonnes of Welsh slate were

used to decorate the Senedd, as well as many tonnes of Welsh oak for the circular debating chamber which houses the sixty Assembly Members. The building has excellent environmental credentials (considering it is essentially a glass box) with heating partly provided by geothermal energy (some twenty-seven pipes run a hundred metres underground to provide this) and rainwater being collected from the immense steel roof to flush the toilets. What is good is that the public can access the viewing gallery (behind security glass) at any time to see the debate below. The rooms and building have all been named in Welsh with the Neuadd (Hall), Siambr (Chamber), Oriel (Gallery) etc. The Oriel is probably the most successful piece of design with an

elegant organic form of Western Red Cedar for the ceiling, imported from Canada, and glass flooring down to the Siambr and committee rooms below.

Around the turn of the millennium, Wales felt like it was being renewed, and the best architects of the world were working on projects here. Zaha Hadid designed an Opera House for Cardiff which, although never built, was replaced with the much-loved 'Armadillo' of the Wales Millennium Centre. Norman Foster was creating his remarkable Great Glasshouse at the National Botanic Gardens, and Richard Rogers won the competition to design the first new government chamber for Wales in centuries. This period of spending and renewal has left Wales with a collection of world-class architecture of which

we can be proud. But buildings aside, it is what happens in them that really matters and Wales can be even prouder that it achieved a level of democracy and independence, not to mention that the centre of power has shifted from Westminster to a fine glass cube on the edge of the Cardiff waterfront.

The Great
Glasshouse

Largest single-span glasshouse in the world

The turn of the millennium felt like a good time to be in Wales. For the first time in centuries the country was gaining some autonomy, the economy was growing, and exciting new architecture projects were under way. Wales was gaining an architectural confidence, with Richard Rogers designing the Senedd, Zaha Hadid designing an Opera House for Cardiff, a whole new 'capital' on show in Cardiff Bay and even in rural Carmarthenshire Norman Foster was opening the world's

most impressive glasshouse for the new National Botanic Garden of Wales at Llanarthne. We've chosen to include that greenhouse as one of the 50 buildings that built Wales as it represents the architectural confidence that the nation was exhibiting as we moved into the twenty-first century.

It can't be cheap to engage Foster + Partners to design your new building, and this was certainly no vanity or tokenistic project; instead it has become a landmark structure that has benefitted both Wales' architectural standing as well as that of the Foster firm. Funded by the National Assembly for Wales, the UK Millennium Fund and other sources, the design is interesting in that it appears very simple

The Great Glasshouse

People: Norman Foster (born 1935), architect; Kathryn Gustafson (born 1951), landscape architect.

Place: A remarkable glass dome 'bubble' that appears to rise out of the Carmarthenshire landscape at the heart of the National Botanic Garden of Wales, built 1999-2003.

Event: Britain's first national botanic garden for 200 years was executed with style and enthusiasm using the world's biggest names in architecture and landscape design, making the glasshouse iconic of millennial optimism in Wales.

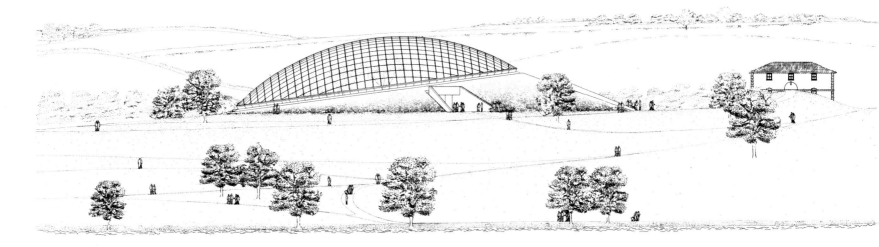

(a bubble of glass among the rolling hillocks) yet it is, in fact, the result of a very clever and complicated piece of engineering. The glasshouse, commissioned in 1995, forms the centrepiece of the 230-hectare site, itself a brave undertaking as it was Europe's first new botanic garden project in decades. The glasshouse is designed to be home to around a thousand Mediterranean-climate plant species, again reflecting confidence that the climate of the sunny Mediterranean could be replicated in Wales. A computer system constantly monitors heat and humidity and opens and closes the roof windows accordingly. Heat comes from a biomass boiler in the Energy Centre which runs on timber trimmings, giving the project an approximately carbon neutral status. Rainwater from the roof is used for irrigation and sewage is treated on site with a natural reed-bed system. The glasshouse has good green credentials, as you'd expect from a major millennial project. Its chief success, however, is as a remarkable piece of structural engineering.

The glasshouse is elliptical in plan and rises organically from the hillside as if it has been inflated with air. The toroidal roof holds almost eight hundred panes of glass (mostly 4m x 1.5m each) and is approximately a hundred metres long and fifty wide, rising from a concrete ring beam up some fifteen metres to the apex of the dome. The substantial concrete substructure required to anchor this 'unsupported' structure has been banked over and turfed, making the three entrances appear to be cut discreetly into the hillside and possibly reminding us of the cheerful home of the Teletubbies. A café and service rooms also nestle into this bank, leaving the main greenhouse span clear for an attractively landscaped interior by Kathryn Gustafson. Substantial fans in the roof help recreate windy Mediterranean climates. Sir Norman Foster said of his work:

'Glasshouses have captured the imagination of generations of architects... the challenge was to find a form that would not only be structurally economical – that would do 'the most with least' – but one that would also fit seamlessly into the natural landscape.'

What Foster created at Llanarthne was a centre-piece to the National Botanic Garden that the people of Wales could 'latch onto' when they thought about the site. People want more than simply gardens to visit these days when they visit a major horticultural attraction. The Eden Project in Cornwall is defined by its greenhouses in the same way that the Great Glasshouse at the Botanic in Wales has become iconic. Visitors come to marvel at the structure as much as the plants inside, and it is a popular venue for public functions and weddings. The Great Glasshouse was, and still is at the time of writing, the largest single-span glasshouse in the world, but it doesn't need a superlative to make you want to visit. Even had it been the second or third largest we'd still love it because it is a truly great piece of architecture, and one that confirmed that the new Wales had arrived on the international architecture scene.

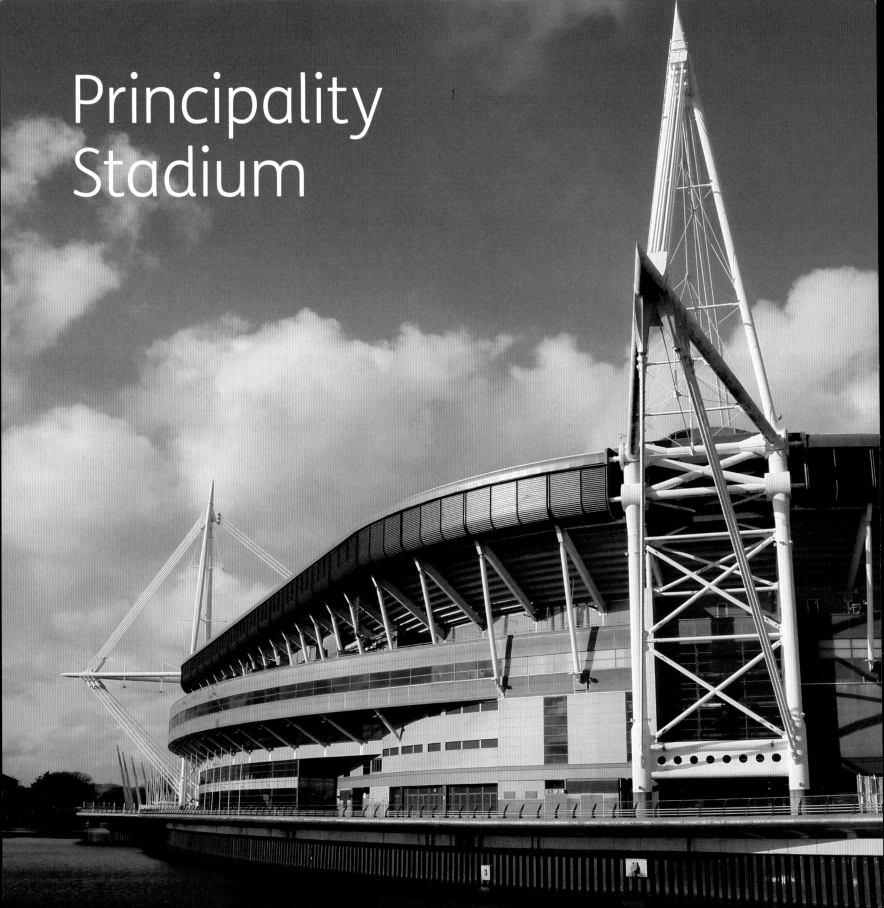

Principality
Stadium

The Welsh love rugby, the national sport that has become indelibly associated with people's perception of Wales. If a Welshman travels abroad, one of the first few questions he gets asked will be about 'the rugby'. Rugby is arguably the most popular game in Wales, loved especially in south Wales, and as a sport it has formed the popular perception of the Welsh in the minds of others. Ask a stranger what a Welshman looks like, and many will think of a stocky rugby player in a red sports kit. The home of national rugby in Wales is Cardiff's riverside Principality Stadium that today sits adjacent to Cardiff Arms Park, approximately on the site of Wales' also much-loved former National Stadium.

The park, originally a piece of undrained swampy ground, was the area behind the Cardiff Arms Hotel. By 1878 the ancient hotel had been demolished and the owner of the site, the third Marquess of Bute, stipulated that the ground could only be used for recreational purposes. In 1881 the first stands were constructed at the site which had a cricket ground and rugby pitch. The site was redeveloped every few decades with numerous buildings until the landmark National Stadium of Wales, informally if somewhat confusingly, known as The Arms Park, was gradually constructed to a 1962 design. The impressive 'claw-like' bowl was constructed in phases between 1970-1984 to hold 65,000 fans, a number reduced to 53,000 after the publication of the Taylor Report in 1990. This much-loved concrete landmark had a short life, though one stand has survived the demolition to be incorporated in today's Principality Stadium.

Principality Stadium

People: John Patrick Crichton-Stuart (1847-1900), Third Marquess of Bute; Bligh Lobb Sports Architecture, architects; W. S. Atkins, structural engineers; John Laing Group, construction team.

Place: The Millennium Stadium, currently known as the Principality Stadium for sponsorship purposes, is the national stadium of Wales in Cardiff. It is a typical piece of millennial contemporary architecture built in time for the 1999 Rugby World Cup in Wales.

Event: Wales and rugby are indelibly linked, and the home of Welsh rugby is undoubtedly the Principality Stadium. It is the place, on match day, that you truly feel the energy and enthusiasm that the Welsh have for their national sport.

The former National Stadium, built of reinforced concrete, was an interesting piece of architecture in itself but too small for the growing numbers who wanted to attend major rugby matches. There was a suggestion that it might be protected as a Listed Building when demolition was suggested in 1997, and that such an expensive building would last only thirteen years after completion possibly showed poor foresight. A swathe of other buildings were also demolished to make way for the new stadium development including the remarkable Empire Pool, one of Wales' greatest buildings of the twentieth century, and one which itself

It seats an impressive 74,500 people and is the second largest stadium in the world with a fully retractable roof

should have been protected by Listed Building status.

The Principality Stadium was built between 1997-1999, changing the axis of the pitch to a north-south alignment from the previous east-west and adding a retractable roof. It opened in June 1999 just in time to host the 1999 Rugby World Cup, and Cardiff also gained two five-star hotels at the same time for the same reason (though neither retain the status today). Today the stadium is home to the national rugby team of Wales but is also used for all manner of events where huge capacity is required, such as music concerts, football matches, boxing and even motorsports. It gave Wales a world-class events venue that, if anything, was over-scaled for a city of Cardiff's size.

The stadium was designed by a team led by architects Bligh Lobb Sports Architecture for a budget of £121 million (£46 million of which came from the Millennium Commission). It seats an impressive 74,500 people and is the second largest stadium in the world with a fully retractable roof. This roof was a great talking point at the time as it was only the second stadium in Europe to be furnished with such technology. It also boasted a palletised playing surface which could be removed when the stadium was hosting non-sporting events. However, following difficulty in maintaining a surface of the required strength and durability, as evinced by some rather embarrassing television footage of international rugby being played on what looked like a rumpled green carpet, this was changed in 2014 in favour of a fixed hybrid surface of grass turf and artificial fibres. The stadium itself rises over three steep tiers and is supported by four impressive ninety metre white masts, all of which serves to bring even the furthest flung spectator as close to the action as possible. Although not the most elegant of recent stadia, it creates an impressive picture when viewed from over the river. The use of 56,000 tonnes of concrete gave it an immense carbon footprint.

The many bars are fitted with special fast-dispensing beer taps, as during one match fans can consume upwards of 75,000 pints of beer, approximately twice the typical 'per head consumption' at comparable Twickenham. There is even a resident hawk named 'Dad' employed to drive pigeons out of the stadium. The substantial redevelopment included an uninspired 'bolted-on' box of a gym, restaurant and cinema on one end. Nearby is an inspired riverfront walkway.

Take a visit to Cardiff on a match day and you'll discover the passion that the Welsh feel for rugby. The position of the stadium in the centre of town is unusual among stadia, but it is a planning success as fans travel in by public transport and bring the entire centre to life with tens of thousands of extra visitors. It has had an immense impact on the economy and atmosphere of the capital, keeping the national sport well and truly in the heart of the city. The surrounding pubs and restaurants literally buzz with the noise and excitement created when a match is on. Even if you don't enjoy watching sport, take a trip to the Principality Stadium one day just to feel that buzz, as to do so is to discover an important part of what Wales is all about.

Greg Stevenson

Dr Greg Stevenson is an architectural historian and Research Fellow of the University of Wales, where he lectured in the history of Welsh architecture at Lampeter. Known to viewers of S4C television for his series series *Y Tŷ Cymreig* and *Y Dref Gymreig*, Greg has authored or co-authored several architecture books including *Cartrefi Cymreig / Welsh Homes*, *Cartrefi Cefn Gwlad Cymru / Houses of the Welsh Countryside*, *Palaces for the People*, *The 1930s Home* etc. He restores vernacular and traditional buildings across Europe for Under the Thatch.

Mark Baker

Dr. Mark Baker is an architectural historian based in Wales. He read History and Archaeology at Bangor University, and Medieval British Studies at Cardiff University, where he also completed his doctoral thesis on *The Development of the Welsh Country House* in 2015. This was funded by the Society of Architectural Historians of Great Britain. As a freelance architectural historian, researcher and writer, Mark has worked with organisations such as the National Trust, Cadw, Royal Commission on Ancient and Historical Monuments of Wales, building preservation trusts and private house owners.

David Wilson

David Wilson is a fine art photographer who strives in his work to capture the beguiling coast and countryside of his native Wales. His images depict the breath-taking beauty and raw majesty of a land and seascape sculpted by extreme elements and partially shaped by man. His acclaimed books include; *Pembrokeshire*, an homage to his home county, *Wales – A Photographer's Journey*, an epic visual travelogue of an enchanting country, and *The Starlings & Other Stories*, a unique collaboration with some of the finest crime fiction writers in Britain.

Thanks

In particular we'd like to thank Philip Hobson at Cadw for providing the Listed building reports on many of the buildings, Phil Davies of Cyngor Llyfrau Cymru for information on Castell Brychan, and Katy Stevenson for suggesting we include Tredegar Central Surgery. Thanks to Fernando Williams for providing the photographs of Capel Bethel in Patagonia and Keith Morris / Eisteddfod Genedlaethol Cymru for the images of Y Pafiliwn.

Credits

50 Buildings That Built Wales Published in Great Britain in 2016 by Graffeg Limited.

Written by Greg Stevenson and Mark Baker copyright © 2016.
Photography by David Wilson copyright © 2016 and other photographers.
Designed and produced by Graffeg Limited copyright © 2016

Graffeg Limited, 24 Stradey Park Business Centre, Mwrwg Road, Llangennech, Llanelli, Carmarthenshire SA14 8YP Wales UK Tel 01554 824000 www.graffeg.com

The publisher gratefully acknowledges the financial support of the Welsh Books Council.

ISBN 9781905582808

1 2 3 4 5 6 7 8 9

Photo credits

©Aled Llywelyn / National Eisteddfod Wales: page 150

©Allen R. Lloyd: pages 106-107, 108

©Amgueddfa Cymru – National Museum Wales: page 83 (middle, bottom)

©Antonia Dewhurst: pages 143, 144, 147

©Chris Jones-Jenkins 1994: page 57

©Christopher Jones / Alamy Stock Photo: page 178

©Cornelia Bayley: pages 62, 64 (bottom left and right)

©Country Life: pages 60, 63

©Crown copyright (2016) Visit Wales: pages 20, 38, 39, 40, 89, 132, 151 (bottom right)

©CW Images / Alamy Stock Photo: page 114

©David Angel / Alamy Stock Photo: page 98

©David Wilson: pages 6, 7, 8, 9, 14, 15, 16, 17, 18, 22, 23, 24, 25, 26, 27, 28, 29, 34, 35, 36, 38, 42, 46, 47, 48, 49, 50, 51, 52, 54, 56, 58, 59, 66, 67, 70, 71 (top), 72, 73, 82, 83 (top), 84, 85, 88, 90, 100, 101, 102, 103, 104, 105, 110, 111, 112, 113, 116, 117, 118, 122, 124, 125, 126, 127, 128, 129, 130, 131, 133, 134, 135, 136, 137, 140, 141 (right top, right bottom), 142, 145, 146, 152, 154, 158, 161, 162, 163, 164, 165, 170, 174 (top, bottom right), 176, 179, 180, 181, 182, 183, 184, 185, 186, 187, 188, 189, 190, 193, 196, 197, 198, 199, 200, 201, 202, 203, 204, 205, 206, 207, 208, 210

©Dickon Fetherstonhaugh: pages 32, 119, 121 (middle)

©EduWales / Alamy Stock Photo: page 172

©Elaine Davey: pages 78, 81

©f22photography / Alamy Stock Photo: page 194

©Fernando Williams: pages 166, 167, 168, 169

©Foster + Partners: page 209

©Geoff Abbott / Alamy Stock Photo: page 141 (left)

©Geoff Charles / National Library Wales: page 156

©Glamorgan Archives: page 19

©Greg Stevenson: pages 68, 69

©Gwrych Castle Preservation Trust: pages 95, 96, 97, 120, 121 (top, bottom)

©Gwynedd Council: page 13

©Huw Jones / Photolibrary Wales: page 86

©Jim Clark / Alamy Stock Photo: page 33

©Jonathan Myles-Lea: page 64 (top)

©Justin Kase Ztwoz / Alamy Stock Photo: pages 138-139

©Keith Morris News / Alamy Stock Photo: page 171

©Keith Morris / National Eisteddfod Wales: pages 148, 151 (bottom left)

©Landscape / Alamy Stock Photo: page 109

©LatitudeStock / Alamy Stock Photo: page 61, 65

©Liquid Light / Alamy Stock Photo: page 115

©Loop Images Ltd / Alamy Stock Photo: page 30

©Mark Baker: pages 74, 75 (bottom), 76, 77

©MARKA / Alamy Stock Photo: page 151 (top)

©Matt Emmett: page 94

©Matthew Jenkins: pages 191, 192

©Media Wales Ltd: pages 37, 44, 45

©Michael Dunlea / Alamy Stock Photo: page 75 (top)

©Michael Olivers / Alamy Stock Photo: pages 53, 55

©National Library Wales: pages 91 (top right), 92, 93

©Nora Summers / Dylan's Bookstore: page 87

©Paul Mattock / Photolibrary Wales: page 31

©The Photolibrary Wales / Alamy Stock Photo: pages 21 (top, bottom), 212

©Portmeirion Ltd: page 71 (bottom)

©Prifysgol Bangor / Bangor University: pages 173, 174 (bottom left), 175

©Sebastian Wasek / Alamy Stock Photo: pages 10, 11

©Steve Vidler / Alamy Stock Photo: page 12

©Wellcome Library, London: page 91 (bottom left)